UNDERSTANDING THE NEW TESTAMENT

DEDICATION

*In gratitude to
the community of Pope John XXIII Seminary,
Weston, Massachusetts,
who have been a living Gospel for me
for seventeen years.*

CATHOLIC
HOME LIBRARY

UNDERSTANDING
THE NEW TESTAMENT

Stephen Doyle, OFM

FC Books
Los Angeles

PRESIDENT:
Fr. Anthony Scannell, Capuchin

EDITORS:
Gary Bradley, MA; Robert Delaney, STD
Corinne Hart, PhD; Karl Holtsnider.

SERIES CONSULTANTS:
Rev. Francis Colborn, STD
Rev. James Gehl, MA, M.Div.
Alexis Navarro, PhD

ART and PHOTOGRAPHY:
Art Director: Robert Miller
Graphic Assistance: Rick Byrum,
Christine Soldenski
Photo Editors: Lucy Liu Brown, MCA
Russell Richards
Staff Photographers: Michael McBlane,
Jack Quinn, SJ, Catherine Busch,
Edd Anthony, OFM.

EDITORIAL ASSISTANCE:
Rev. Elmer Carroll, SJ; Elizabeth Montes
Rev. C. Vincent Peterson, MA
Sister Patricia Rocap, BVM
Brother Kevin Schroeder, OFM
Loretta Hernandez, Peg Bradley,
Rose Delaney, Christi Montes.

MARKETING:
Direction/Research: William Sheck,
Jose Velasquez, Helen Payne
Assistance: Eloise Evans, Blanca Gallegos,
Dorla Lord, Rev. John MacDonell, OFM
Ann Palacio, Patrice Russell, Rosita Steer,
Adela Stewart, Ida DeGeorge,
Yolanda Young.

With ecclesiastical approval:
Most Reverend Roger M. Mahony
Archbishop of Los Angeles
July 18, 1988

© 1989 Franciscan Communications

Library of Congress
Catalog Card Number: 88-82197.
ISBN 1-55-944-000-7

COVER PHOTO: Jesus said to them, "Come follow me, and I will make you fishers of my people." (cf. Mark 1:17)

CATHOLIC HOME LIBRARY books make available in an informative and inspiring way the riches of church teaching and practice as they have developed since the Second Vatican Council.

For more information please contact:
Franciscan Communications
1229 S. Santee Street
Los Angeles, CA 90015
(213) 746-2916 / (800) 421-8510

Printed in Singapore
by Singapore National Printers Ltd.

CONTENTS

UNDERSTANDING THE BASICS

Testament

For most people "testament" is only half a phrase. From their experience it goes with "Last will and...." For the early Christian community it had just that meaning. "Someone loved me enough to promise to leave me something of value after his death." The first believers felt very comfortable in calling their writings a testament because they spoke of God's promise fulfilled in the life, death and resurrection of God's Son. "To as many as received him he gave the power to become

(photo right) The Roman coliseum: site of public events in early Christian times.

the children of God" (John 1:12). Life in Christ is the Father's legacy. It is the life of grace, light and love. The Greek word for testament also means covenant: a communion of people with God, a loving, faithful relationship. This is the relationship to which God has called us from the time of Abraham, our father in faith, who came to be known as the "friend" of God (James 2:23). A thousand years later, by the time of Jeremiah the prophet, the people were so unfaithful to that first Covenant that the prophet says: "The days are coming, says the Lord, when I will make a New Covenant with the house of Israel and the house of Judah" (Jeremiah 31:31).

Old Testament

For the first generation of Christians there was no other Bible except the Hebrew Scriptures, the Old Testament. When they searched them seeking to find the meaning of Jesus and themselves, when they pondered the words of the prophets, they found themselves - but as the people of the New Covenant. The new writings that spoke of their Lord, of themselves and of their experiences thus came to be called the books of the New Covenant, or the New Testament.

"New," however, can be misleading. It is usually contrasted to what is "Old," no longer useful. The implication is that it can be thrown away or discarded. Not so. Neither God's Word, God's promise nor God's people have ever been or will be discarded. The New Testament is "new" in the sense that we speak of a "new" branch on a tree or a flower on a plant. Neither branch nor flower could come to be without the tree or plant. According to the Bible,

God had made one covenant after another with God's people. This was done first through Abraham, and then through Moses and David until finally God covenanted us through Jesus, who is called the "branch" or "shoot" of David. Without God's Word to, and Covenant with, the Jewish people, we would be rootless and die. Indeed even the great Paul did not see himself as discarding the Old Testament, but rather experiencing its flowering in the New. "Consider that you do not support the root, the root supports you" (Romans 11:18).

New Testament

When Jesus gave his people the message of the New Covenant he told them to go forth and preach, making disciples of all nations (Matthew 28:19). He never told them to write, and didn't even bother to do so himself. How is it that we now have a book called the "New Testament"?

Despite the fact that we find the Gospels first in it, they were not the first writings. That honor goes to the letters of Paul. They were written because the people to whom he had brought the faith were having trouble living out their faith. Today we can be grateful for their troubles, for without them we would not have the letters of Paul. The situation was not unlike the "Dear Abby" columns in our newspapers. But in her columns, Abby prints the letter and then her answer. Usually with Paul, we only have his answer and have to read between the lines to search out the question.

And questions and problems there were in the early community of Christians. People today think that tension in the Church started in the 1960's with Vatican Council II. It started with the resurrection, and the New Testament letters were written to show people how to handle it. That is why those answers can still speak to our own tensions and struggles today.

The Gospels arrived late on the scene. The first of them, Mark, was written about forty years after the resurrection. The early community didn't need written documents when they had the living word of those who were

enthusiastic witnesses to Jesus. When the Gospel was finally written down because the first witnesses were dying off, it was not meant to be a life of Jesus, but rather, a call to life in Jesus, an invitation to discipleship.

The rest of the New Testament, the Acts of the Apostles, the catholic epistles and the book of Revelation all speak to us of life in the early community, its struggles, tensions and identity crises.

Through all of them, God speaks to us today, for the same Holy Spirit who inspired those who wrote, inspires those who read. That is why the Scriptures must be read not only with understanding and insight, but also with prayer. Any other book can be read, and the only response necessary is whether or not it was interesting. God's Word is an invitation with an R.S.V.P. attached. Either we will follow God or we won't, but the decision first requires prayer. That is why the Bible is such a unique book. And if we read it prayerfully often enough, we won't just find the story of Jesus there - we'll find our own story.

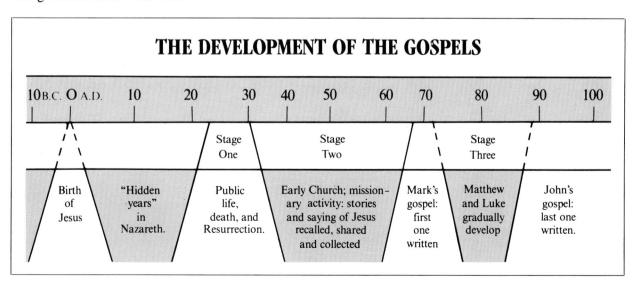

THE DEVELOPMENT OF THE GOSPELS

10 B.C. O A.D.	10	20	30	40	50	60	70	80	90	100
			Stage One		Stage Two			Stage Three		
Birth of Jesus	"Hidden years" in Nazareth.		Public life, death, and Resurrection.	Early Church; missionary activity: stories and saying of Jesus recalled, shared and collected			Mark's gospel: first one written	Matthew and Luke gradually develop		John's gospel: last one written.

If we read the Bible prayerfully enough, we won't just find the story of Jesus there - we'll find our own story.

Gospels

If you have ever taken a course in literature you noticed how many literary forms (means for conveying truth or ideas) there are: prose, poetry, history, editorial, essay, biography, humor, novel, short story, propaganda - to mention just a few. You come across many of them just by perusing your daily newspaper. They have been used by writers for centuries to get across their ideas.

There is one literary form, however, that is absolutely unique: gospel. It is unique because the person it centers on is unique: Jesus Christ. It is unique because it demands a response. Many people think that the closest literary form to gospel is biography. Far from it. The closest literary form is an invitation with an R.S.V.P. The Gospel is an invitation to accept Jesus, to come

to know him and to live our lives with him. The Gospel is nothing more and nothing less than an expansion and explanation of his words "Come, follow me" (Matthew 4:19).

There was a time after the ascension of Jesus when the Gospel was not written. The time lasted about forty years (the biblical period for a generation). The first generation of Christians didn't need or want a gospel. Those who followed Jesus and had heard, and lived with, and seen the risen Lord were still among them. The Gospel was the very life of the early Christians. That is why the statement is still true today: "The only Gospel some people will ever read is the one you write with your life."

The time came, however, around the year 70 A.D. when the first generation of disciples was being martyred for their belief in the Gospel or was being gathered to the Lord. Already in the mid-fifty's Paul could write that Jesus "appeared to Kephas, then to the twelve. After that he appeared to more than five hundred disciples at once, most of whom are still living, though some have fallen asleep" (1 Corinthians 15:5-6).

Thus the living Gospel had to become the written Gospel. Another reason why this had to be was that, as with all famous people, some fantastic and spurious stories began circulating about Jesus. Some were silly like the one that told of the boy Jesus making birds out of clay and commanding them to fly away, and they did. Others were dangerous and destructive of Jesus and what he came to do, like those that insisted he was an apparition and not really human like us. The Church knew "he had to become like all of us in every way, that he might be a faithful and merciful high priest before God"

"You are of God, you little ones..." (1 John 4:4).

(Hebrews 2:17). The very truth of our salvation was in jeopardy if the stories about Jesus not really being human were also true. The Church knew he was truly God and truly human and wrote the Gospel to insist on it.

There was a third reason for writing. The early Christians believed that what they prayed for so fervently in the Lord's prayer, "thy kingdom come, thy will be done on earth" (Matthew 6:10), would occur in their own life time. They didn't see any need for a written Gospel if the second coming of Jesus was imminent. When it didn't occur after several decades, they were not certain when it would be and decided to put the Gospel in writing until it did occur.

The Romans used to call the Mediterranean, "our sea." The generation of disciples after Jesus could also call it, "our sea." There were communities (Churches) of followers of "the Way" (Acts 9:2) all around it. The Gospel had been preached and accepted in Alexandria (N. Africa), Palestine, Syria, present-day Turkey and Greece,

all the way to Rome. But there were people of different ethnic backgrounds, cultures, thought patterns and dreams. The Gospel had to take root in each of them and be adapted to them. What Pope Paul VI had to say about evangelization today was not less true then: "Evangelization loses much of its force and effectiveness if it does not take into consideration the actual people to whom it is addressed, if it does not use their language, their signs and symbols, if it does not answer the questions they ask, and if it does not have an impact on their concrete life" (On Evangelization in the Modern World 1976).

Because the Gospel is for everyone, it had to become Gospels. Good pastors that they were, Matthew, Mark, Luke and John, each in their own unique way showed that Jesus is the answer. They each gathered the material handed on to them as individual stories in the life and voice of the Church, and they each arranged and interpreted it to suit the needs of their respective communities.

WHAT DOES THE CHURCH SAY ABOUT HOW TO UNDERSTAND THE GOSPELS?

In order to determine correctly the trustworthiness of what is transmitted in the Gospels, the interpreter must take careful note of the three stages of tradition by which the teaching and the life of Jesus have come down to us.

30-33 AD

FIRST STAGE: Christ our Lord attached to himself certain chosen disciples who had followed him from the beginning, who had seen his works and had heard his words, and thus were qualified to become witnesses of his life and teaching.

33-70 AD

SECOND STAGE: The Life and Preaching of the Church. The apostles, bearing testimony of Jesus, proclaimed first and foremost the death and resurrection of the Lord, faithfully recounting his life and words, and in regard to the manner of their preaching, taking into account the circumstances of their hearers.... The apostles, when handing on to their hearers the things which in actual fact the Lord had said and done, did so in the light of that fuller understanding which they enjoyed as a result of being schooled by the glorious things being accomplished in Christ and of being illumined by the Spirit of Truth.... Now, they interpreted his words and deeds according to the needs of their hearers.

70-90 AD

THIRD STAGE: The Writing of the four Gospels. The sacred authors (evangelists), for the benefit of the Churches, took this earliest body of instruction which had been handed on orally at first, and then in writing,...and set it down in the four Gospels.... Each followed a method suitable to the purpose which he had in view. They selected certain things out of the many that had been handed on; some they synthesized, some they explained with an eye to the situation of the Churches.... The sacred authors selected especially those items which were adapted to the varied circumstances of the faithful, as well as the end which they themselves wished to attain.... Interpreters must ask themselves what the evangelists intended by recounting a saying or fact in a certain way or by placing it in a certain context.

Statement of the Pontifical Biblical Commission, approved by Pope Paul VI April 21, 1964

It should be no surprise that the Gospels differ as to WHERE (Matthew's Sermon on the Mount versus Luke's Sermon on the Plain) or WHEN (John has the cleansing of the temple at the beginning of his Gospel, the others at the end) an event occurred. Their interest was in a person, not in a map or calendar. John sums up well what a Gospel is for: "These are written that you may believe that Jesus is the Messiah, the Son of God, and that by believing you might have life in his name" (John 20:31).

The Synoptics

In a recent election a candidate dropped out when it was found that he had plagiarized (borrowed without acknowledging the source) from the speech of another politician. When a student writes a term paper and the teacher recognizes that he or she has read the identical or similar material in another book, the teacher will suspect plagiarism. He will put the two side by side to see if one depends on the other.

Synoptic comes from the Greek word meaning "to see side by side." For years scholars have known that when they put the first three gospels side by side a dependence is obvious. Both Matthew and Luke borrowed from Mark, giving rise to great similarities among them. That is why they are called the "Synoptic" Gospels.

Mark would never have been dismayed nor have accused them of plagiarism. He would have been delighted that they thought enough of his Gospel to adapt it to the needs of their communities.

Matthew and Luke, seen together, contain much other material in common not included in Mark. It is believed that they both borrowed from an early catechetical document, called "Q," (source) containing many teachings of Jesus. In addition, both Matthew and Luke had their own "private stock" of things that Jesus said and did that were handed on only in their own Churches. Since each used the material in his own way for the unique needs of his particular communities, a comparison can be very helpful for a deeper understanding of the Gospels. A good Bible will have cross references to parallel passages to help the reader get more out of God's Word.

THE GOSPEL ACCORDING TO MARK

The Pioneer in Writing a Gospel

I f you have ever awakened in the morning, burdened with problems, difficulties and tensions, then Mark's Gospel was written for you. If you have ever picked up the paper with its news of crime, war and treachery and been depressed by a senseless world, then Mark's Gospel was written for you. If you have ever been betrayed by a friend or maligned by a relative, then Mark's Gospel was written for you. If you have ever faced a day when it seemed like even God had given up and didn't want to get involved anymore with the mess we had made of things, then Mark's Gospel was written for you. If you have come to a point where the most sincere prayer you can muster is, "God help us," then Mark's Gospel was written for you.

Mark wrote for a troubled, suffering community. They had converted to the "Way" (the earliest name for Christianity - Acts 9:2) because they thought it was the way to peace, satisfaction and happiness. People don't convert from one way of life or religion or philosophy to another if they find their present situation fulfilling. It is when that fulfillment is lacking that they look for something else. For Mark's community, that something else was Jesus. As even today's bumper stickers proclaim: "Jesus is the Answer." Or so they thought. They turned from the dissatisfaction and lack of fulfillment of their old ways and responded to the call to follow Jesus.

Response to Problems

Jesus was preached to them as Messiah. Some misinterpreted what that meant. Turning to Jesus didn't take away all of their problems. Indeed they seemed to be suffering more than ever just because they had turned to Jesus. Some of their community had even been put to death for their faith. Many of them felt disillusioned and disappointed.

They cried, "God help us," and God answered with Mark's Gospel. In the very first line he tells them that there is Gospel, i.e., Good News. And the Good News is that God does help us. The Good News is that God is with us in Jesus. The Good News is that no matter what, Jesus is among us. But Mark doesn't give them the Good News that they wanted to hear. They wanted to hear that the time had arrived when God would "wipe every tear from their

THE HEART OF MARK'S GOSPEL: 8:34-38

Jesus summoned the crowd with his disciples and said to them: "Whoever wishes to come after me, must deny his very self, take up his cross, and follow in my steps. Whoever would preserve her life will lose it, but whoever loses her life for my sake and the Gospel's will preserve it. What profit is there for one to gain the whole world and forfeit one's life? What could one give in exchange for one's life? Whoever is ashamed of me and of my words in this faithless and sinful generation, the Son of Man will be ashamed of when he comes in his Father's glory with the holy angels."

Mark writes for a community discouraged and dismayed with their present suffering.

eyes and there would be no more death or mourning, wailing or pain" (Revelation 21:4). No, Mark's Good News is not that Jesus came to give us life without lumps. It is that he knows what we are going through, because he went through it himself. And he not only knows what cross we bear, but he is bearing it with us.

Mark is writing for a community discouraged and dismayed with their present suffering. They yearn for the transfigured and transformed risen Jesus to establish the Reign of God in glory. Mark reminds them that even Jesus did not have the resurrection without previously having the cross. Neither will they. But they won't be alone in bearing it.

Mark's message is the same as the story that has made the rounds in recent years: "Footprints in the Sand," the story of someone who dreamed that he had seen his life passing before him. At almost every instance he saw the footprints of Jesus beside his own in the sand. But at crucial times of tension, sorrow and suffering, he saw only one set of footprints on the beach and asked

why Jesus had abandoned him. The reply: "My child, I love you and I would never leave you. During the times of trial and suffering, when you saw only one set of footprints, it was then that I carried you."

The Cross of Humanity

But if Mark speaks of Jesus bearing the cross, it is not just the cross of Calvary and the Way of the Cross. It is the cross of being human and suffering the wounds of our weakened humanity. The author of Hebrews writes that Jesus "had to become like all of us in every way, that he might be a merciful and faithful high priest before God to expiate the sins of the people. Because he himself was tested through what he suffered, he is able to help those who are being tested" (Hebrews 2:17).

Already in chapter 2 of Mark, the cross appears when Jesus has to bear the suspicions and accusations of the religious authorities who should have known better. Then he is questioned as to why he doesn't fast, and shortly thereafter he has to answer the charge

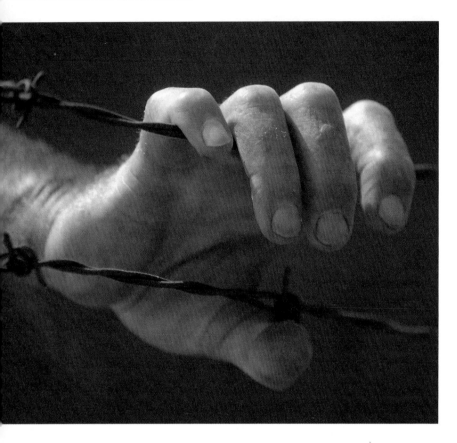

"He has sent me to proclaim liberty to captives...to let the oppressed go free" (Luke:4:18).

that his disciples were irreligious because they picked grain on the sabbath. In the next chapter Jesus is accused of blasphemy for healing on the sabbath. He has to call for a boat as the crowd pushes in on him, and then some say he is mentally unbalanced while others say he is possessed by the devil. In chapter 4 Jesus has to deal with the dullness of his best friends who can't even comprehend what he says plainly. In the midst of a storm these same friends accuse him of being indifferent and uncaring. And so it goes. The cross of suspicion, mockery, accusation, betrayal, abandonment, misunderstanding, weariness, loneliness, frustration and indifference is the one he bears. Indeed he was like us in every way.

Mark begins by saying that he is writing the Gospel of Jesus Christ, the Son of God. Then he proceeds to show how human, weak and wounded Jesus was. The paradox of Jesus is the dilemma of each of us, bearing "the slings and arrows of outrageous fortune," as Shakespeare says, yet headed for the Reign of God in the footsteps of Jesus. How often have you heard the anxious voice of a child on a trip saying, "Are we almost there?" The journey of Jesus toward cross and tomb is punctuated with an affirmation to his disciples: "We're almost there." Three times in the course of the narrative he assures them "that the Son of Man must suffer greatly and be rejected by the elders, the chief priests and the scribes and be killed and rise after three days. He spoke this openly" (8:31).

The Price of Prophets

Jesus didn't need a crystal ball to know that he was on a collision course with the political and religious leaders. His rejection at Nazareth (6:1 ff) led him to compare his own fate to that of so many other prophets. Closer to home, in the same chapter, John the Baptist's prophetic candor cost him his head and brought Jesus to the notice of Herod. In the next chapter Jesus takes on the Pharisees. The nicest thing that he says about them is that they are hypocrites who have confused a deep relationship with God with external piety and unfeeling legalism. Mark's Jesus gives no indication that he ever took a course in how to win friends and influence people!

One of the puzzling things about Mark's Gospel is the so called "Messianic Secret." Whenever Jesus is called Messiah or does something marvelous, he tells his audience not to spread it around. This is because of his refusal to live up to the popular but misguided messianic expectations shared even by Peter and the disciples. Their perception of his role is in conflict with the divine will. "Get behind me, Satan. You are thinking not as God does, but as human beings do" (8:33). Those words were not addressed to the Pharisees, but to Peter!

Jesus chose his way. It was the way of the cross. It was not forced on him. He was not a helpless victim of circumstances. The comparison of his

PARABLES

Jesus' favorite way of teaching was by telling stories called parables. Too often, the message is fogged in by not appreciating what a parable is supposed to do. It is not meant to explain, impart knowledge, teach nor much less entertain. Nor is a parable an allegory in which every feature has a corresponding identity in real life. It seems that a favorite pastime of some early church fathers was to make the parables into allegories and miss the point. Thus for Augustine the inn of the Good Samaritan becomes the Church, while the inn-keeper becomes the Pope, the injured man personifies humanity, and the Samaritan is Jesus, and the priest and levite are the Old Testament. If Jesus had heard that explanation he wouldn't have recognized the story, much less the point he was making.

The Word of God is an invitation and the parable is no exception. It is an invitation to put yourself in the story and allow your values to be challenged, your preconceived notions shattered and your priorities tested. But the smug, complacent and comfortable don't want to move from their positions and accept the invitation, if indeed they recognize it as an invitation to themselves. All preachers have had the experience of a person coming up after a sermon and congratulating them for finally saying something to "those people." The hearer seems to know just whom the preacher had in mind, and, of course, it wasn't themselves!

Jesus had the same problem. A parable presupposed openness and faith in the hearer. Many had neither. That is why all four evangelists quote Isaiah who, looking back on his life in frustration and failure, says he was sent that "they may look and see but not perceive, and hear and listen but not understand, in order that they may not be converted and forgiven" (Mark 4:12; Isaiah 6:9). His listeners had missed the point not because the parables deceived them. That wasn't necessary since they had already deceived themselves.

Step into each parable. They are doors leading into the Reign of God. But you need two keys to unlock them, faith and an open heart.

being led like a lamb to the slaughter who opened not his mouth is a limited one indeed. The point is not that he was led, but that he did not cry out in protest at a tragic fate that was forced on him. He was not a passive, helpless lamb. He was a messiah who was a suffering servant: "We thought of him as one smitten by God and afflicted. But he was pierced for our offenses, crushed for our sins. Upon him was the chastisement that makes us whole, by his stripes we were healed" (Isaiah 53:5). And as the servant, Jesus also recognized that if the finger of God was involved in his death, so would it be involved with what would come next: "Because of his affliction, he shall see the light in the fullness of days" (Isaiah 53:11).

Crisis or Opportunity?

On the stage of the passion, the high priest, Pilate, and even Judas are indeed minor characters and merely supporting actors. In the Japanese language, "crisis" also signifies "opportunity." What the witnesses of the passion saw as tragic crisis, Jesus saw as loving opportunity. The early Christians grasped this well when, for the first thousand years in their art, they depicted the figure of Jesus on the cross as living and triumphant. Later generations distorted the message of the cross by depicting Jesus as dead and gruesomely defeated by it. But the cross was good news for Mark's community. Through faith in their Lord, their own sufferings could be transformed from dehumanizing tragedy into glorious triumph. Jesus had showed them how.

In spite of this wonderful message, which indeed is good news for us,

SON OF MAN

Jesus was not fond of the title Messiah or Christ because it was so easily misunderstood by his contemporaries. They wanted a magnificent, triumphing messiah who would subdue their political enemies. To put it in contemporary language, that was not his bag. He much preferred to be known as the "Son of Man."

When he referred to himself this way, his hearers would immediately understand what he was saying about himself. They had read about the "Son of Man" in both Ezechiel and Daniel.

Ezechiel himself was called by God "Son of Man" (2:1) to impress upon him the frailness of his own humanity. He is mere man, just man, only human with all the weakness and vulnerability that the human condition implies. Jesus, the Son of God, embraced this title to convey how fully and completely he identified with us.

Daniel used the title, "Son of Man," to designate the figure who would appear at the time of God's definitive judgment on his people. He was the figure of the end times. When asked by the high priest if he were the Messiah, Jesus replied, "You will see the Son of Man seated at the right hand of the Power" (Mark 14:62). In him, the end time has been inaugurated and God's judgment has begun.

Mark's Gospel has rarely won a popularity contest. It is shorter than the others, gives us less of the life and teachings of Jesus, and Mark's grammar and vocabulary would hardly have given him a high grade on a college entrance examination. He has this in his favor, however, that his portrait of Jesus is alive and real. He did his job so well, gathering and arranging the stories that had been circulating as the living Gospel for forty years, that Matthew and Luke used him as the major source for their Gospels. They took his material and reinterpreted it to answer the needs and solve the problems of their own communities.

Mark would have been happy with that. He knew when he put down his quill, that the final word on Jesus had not yet been spoken. He wanted to introduce us to Jesus. Then it would be up to each one to get to know him, embrace him and accept him as Lord of their lives. Mark did his job and wrote his Gospel. He expects us to write ours.

(photo left) This was the Good News for Mark's community that through faith in their Lord their own sufferings could be transformed from dehumanizing tragedy to glorious triumph.

THE GOSPEL ACCORDING TO MATTHEW

The Scribe "who brings from his storeroom both new and old." (13:52)

When Matthew sat down to write his Gospel he was confronted with a major problem. His community was at each other's throats over what it meant to be a Christian, over who Jesus actually was, over what it meant to be Church, over who had authority to speak in the place of Jesus, over what should be the lifestyle of Christians and over what demands should be placed on those who wanted to join their ranks.

Fifty years after the death of Jesus, Matthew was faced with a problem that Pope Paul VI in our day said was a permanent one for the Church: "The Church is an evangelizer, but begins by being evangelized herself.... She needs to listen unceasingly to her reasons for hoping, to the new commandment of love...if she wishes to retain freshness, vigor and strength in order to proclaim the Gospel" (On Evangelization in the Modern World, 1976). Thus Matthew's problem is our problem. How can we go forth and make disciples of all nations if we're not sure what it means to be a disciple? The evangelizer must first be evangelized, and Matthew took on that role for his community.

Kosher Christianity?

Matthew had to deal with the conservatives who wanted to conserve everything of their Jewish past and find their identity there. They had history on their side. If being Jewish was good enough for Jesus and the twelve apostles, it was good enough for them. Jesus had not rejected Judaism, its

ritual, laws or customs, but only criticized their abuse. He remained Jewish to the end. The conservatives took as their campaign slogan Jesus' words: "Do not think that I have come to abolish the Law or the prophets. I have come not to abolish but to fulfill" (Matthew 5:17).

The practical implications of the conservative stand were many. According to this group those wanting to embrace Jesus had first to embrace Judaism: the kosher laws, the ritual of circumcision for males, strict sabbath observance, etc. To become a Christian meant first to become a Jew. For them, Jesus was just another rabbi with his own distinctive interpretation of the Law. He may have been a reformer but he was certainly not an innovator.

On the other side were the liberals who wanted to be liberated from what they considered the shackles of the past. Some were Jewish converts to Christianity, disillusioned with their previous affiliation and ready to throw it over. Others were Gentile converts who had never experienced Judaism and saw no reason for that to be a condition of

THE HEART OF MATTHEW'S GOSPEL: 13:52

"Every scribe who is learned in the Reign of God is like the head of a household who can bring from his storeroom both the new and the old."

discipleship. For them, Jesus was not a reformer, but an innovator. The Old Testament was exactly that: old and irrelevant.

What the conservatives saw as the essence of being a Christian, the liberals saw as an obstacle to it. For the conservatives, the Gospel was Jesus and the Law. For the others, it was Jesus. Period. Besides, the very rabbis that the conservatives were appealing to were the ones who were knocking the community's belief in Jesus, implying that he was, if not a charlatan, then a fool. At any rate, he wasn't the Messiah, the Son of David. They were also mocking the kind of people who were joining Matthew's community: prostitutes, pimps, the poor, and those ignorant of the intricacies of religious Law. They were the dregs of society, the misfits who couldn't make it anywhere else. And this, the rabbis questioned, was supposed to be the Reign of God?

So the community was pulled apart by tensions within and accusations without. Matthew had a major problem: Where does the Good News fit into all of that?

View from the Top

Matthew's first insight, which provides the framework for his Gospel, is to see that God's plan for salvation is not divided into two eras, old testament and new testament. No, the whole expanse of God's gracious plan in Jesus is threefold:

1. The long period of the time of preparation for Jesus: the time of promises.

2. The life of Jesus up through his redeeming work on the cross: the time of fruition.

3. The work of Jesus continued in the Church from his resurrection to the end of the age: the time of fulfillment.

No one of these eras can exist without the other, any more than a root, plant and flower can exist without each other. The second stage depends upon the first, because Jesus was first of all the Messiah, the fulfillment of all the Jewish hopes. To cut him off from his roots is to misunderstand him. Thus the conservatives are partially right. That is why Matthew starts out his Gospel by saying it is the Good News of Jesus, the Messiah, the Son of David, the Son of Abraham. Jesus cannot be understood without his past.

But so are the liberals partially right as well. The last lines of the Gospel

"Hope is the struggle of the soul, breaking loose from what is perishable and attesting her eternity" (Herman Melville).

proclaim that Jesus' last instruction to his disciples is not that they are to make disciples by teaching them to obey the Jewish Law and be circumcised. No, the Law has lost its power which now resides in the risen Lord, its fulfillment. The power and authority are now elsewhere:

All power in heaven and on earth has been given to me. Go, therefore, and make disciples of all nations, baptizing them in the name of the Father and of the Son and of the Holy Spirit, teaching them to observe all that I have commanded you. And behold, I am with you always, until the end of the age (Matthew 28:18-20).

DISCIPLES

The followers of all rabbis were called disciples.
The followers of Jesus in the Gospels have the same title,
but they are disciples with a big difference.
Compare:

DISCIPLES OF A RABBI	DISCIPLES OF JESUS
They took the initiative to choose the most prestigious teacher.	You have not chosen me, but I have chosen you (John 15:16).
The rabbi accepted only the best and the brightest.	God chose the foolish of this world to shame the wise (1 Corinthians 1:27).
They came to the rabbi only for knowledge. Their only suffering was the drudgery of memorizing the rabbi's opinions.	I am the Way, the Truth, and the Life (John 14:6). Unless you take up your cross daily and follow me, you cannot be my disciple (Luke 9:23).
Other relationships were more important than that to the rabbi.	Unless you prefer me to father and mother you cannot be my disciple (Matthew 10:37).
Their cleverness in argumentation was an advertisement for the prestige of the rabbi.	By this shall all know that you are my disciples, by your love for one another (John 13;35).
After they had learned all they wanted from the rabbi they left him.	Abide in me and you shall bear much fruit (John 15:5).
Then they became rabbis and gathered disciples for themselves.	Preach the Gospel to all nations, making disciples of them (Matthew 28:19).
Discipleship was only open to male Jews.	In Christ Jesus there is neither Jew nor Gentile; nor male or female...for you are all one (Gal 3:28).

Since the identity of the Christian now consists in discipleship to Jesus, the Law which even Jesus observed is now fulfilled. It is superfluous. Jesus had said it was not to be abolished until it was fulfilled. He has done that. He, not the Law, is now the way to God. Jesus Christ is the Good News. The Law is not.

Networking

Christianity, according to Matthew, is dispensed and divorced from the Law; nevertheless, we are not divorced from the God of the Old Testament. He is the God of Abraham, Isaac, Jacob, Moses, David, and all the prophets, as well as being the Father of our Lord Jesus Christ. It was not only John the Baptist who prepared for him. John was only the last of a long line.

When a baby is born, the proud parents usually ask whom you think it looks like. Mother, father, grandparent? Matthew asks us to look at Jesus and see how he resembles all who have gone before him. To the Jewish Christians of his community the genealogy showed Jesus' continuity with the past and identity with the present. Whether the rabbis liked it or not, he is the Son of David.

What seems to us like an exercise in boredom also had a message for the new Gentile members of the community. Matthew mentions four women in the genealogy and they are all non-Jews. Not only that, each one's story shows that they were hardly in the upper bracket of the social register. Tamar seduced her father-in-law. Rahab was a Canaanite who ran a house of ill repute. Ruth was a Moabitess who seduced Boaz. Solomon's mother was Bathsheba who committed adultery with

David. Matthew wants to show through these skeletons in Jesus' closet that, if there was room for such as these in preparing for the Messiah, there's room for the rest of us in the Church to carry on his work.

The story of Jesus' infancy is a telescoping of what had gone before and of what Jesus had fulfilled: all the promises made to the people of Israel, referred to in the Old Testament as "God's Son." Now Jesus is the Son of God and all that was said of Israel can now be said of Jesus.

The infancy narrative also tells us what will be. At his birth, Jesus is ignored by the political and religious leaders, but the Gentiles (Magi) come to him. That is the very thing that is happening in the community for which Matthew is writing. There, many innocent people

Matthew mentions four women in the genealogy of Jesus...each one's story shows they were hardly in the upper bracket of the social register.

The Christians for whom Matthew writes are already suffering for the name of Jesus, just as in the story of the Holy Innocents.

are already suffering for the name of Jesus, just as in the story of the holy innocents; so what's new?

New Moses

Matthew divides the rest of the Good News, up to the passion, into five blocks of material reminiscent of the five books of the Torah attributed to Moses. To reinforce the idea that Jesus is the new and authoritative teacher of God's people, Matthew recalls the picture of Moses on Mount Sinai by placing Jesus on the Mount of Beatitudes where he gives his new teaching. And notice that it is new. He is not just another rabbi who quotes the expert rabbis of the past. He speaks "with authority, and not as one of their scribes" (7:29). If he does quote the commandments, the Law of Moses, it is to go beyond them. "You have heard that it was said 'you shall not commit adultery', but I say to you, everyone who looks at a woman with lust has already committed adultery with her in his heart" (5:27). Jesus' message is one that goes to the heart to transform people from within. The Law can only legislate external behavior. That will often lead to hypocrisy and self-righteousness. That is how Jesus' opponents, the scribes and Pharisees, got such bad reputations as hypocrites.

They set a trap, trying to get Jesus to take sides on which is the greatest commandment. He slips through their legalistic trap by affirming that even God's Word (the Law and the prophets) did not have any meaning without love (22:34).

No, Jesus is not just a rabbi whose opinions are open to debate. With Moses and Elijah, the great teachers of Israel as witnesses, a voice from the heavens declares that Jesus "is my beloved Son, with whom I am well pleased" (Matthew 3:17).

But now, fifty years after the resurrection, where is the voice that Matthew's community should listen to? It was fine to look back and know that Jesus had authority to settle disputes in his lifetime, but where now is that authority in their lifetime to settle their disputes? He did say as his final word, "Behold I am with you always, until the end of the age" (Matthew 28:20).

Here Matthew has gone back to his insight of the threefold division of God's saving plan. In the first age, Moses was the voice of authority. In the second age, Jesus took his place. In the third age, our age, Jesus has passed the prophet's mantle to the Church. If Matthew's community would only open their ears, they would hear the voice of Jesus in Peter, whom Jesus made the "rock" upon which he founded his Church with the authority to bind and loose, the very authority claimed by the rabbis (16:18). In 18:17 that authority is given to the community, the "Church"

(a word found only in Matthew's Gospel), where the risen Lord lives as he promised: "Where two or three are gathered together in my name, there am I in the midst of them" (18:20). This new, third age, is the age of fulfillment. The Law is no longer the binding force of community. Jesus is. Now, with the last words of Jesus to "go forth and evangelize" ringing in their ears, Matthew's community can do just that, but only because Matthew, inspired by the Holy Spirit, has evangelized them. "The Church is an evangelizer but begins by being evangelized." Truer words were never spoken. That is why Matthew wrote his Gospel which still speaks to us today.

"Where two or three are gathered in my name, there am I in the midst of them" (Matthew 18:20).

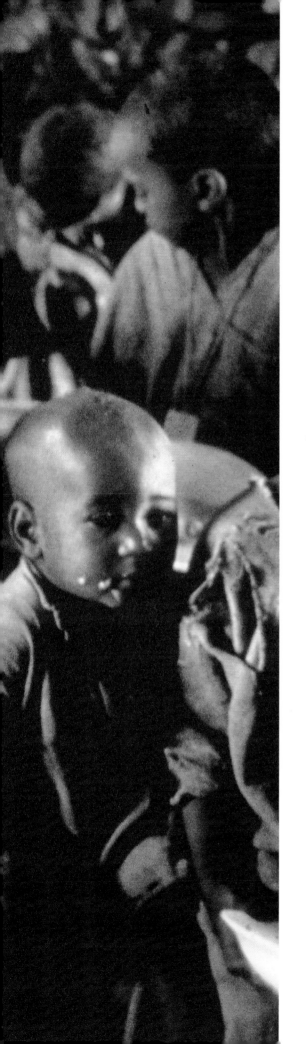

THE GOSPEL ACCORDING TO LUKE

"The Scribe of the Gentleness of Christ" (Dante)

We can't be sure whether Luke ever heard of Matthew's Gospel or ever came across a copy of it. Both Gospels were written around the same time (80 A.D.) and in the same area, Antioch in Syria, where people were first called Christians. Antioch became the new center of the Church after the destruction of Jerusalem in 70 A.D. Even thirty years earlier there had been a strong community of Gentile converts in Antioch before Matthew's Jewish-Christian community fled there as refugees.

But even if Luke had been familiar with Matthew's Gospel, as he was with other "narratives" in circulation (1:1), he could not have used it for his community and would still have had to write his own. The problems of Luke's community were different. They weren't struggling with a Jewish-Christian identity crisis. They were trying to find out what it meant to be Christian in the pagan world of the Roman empire.

Luke's Gospel is addressed (1:3) to a person named Theophilus which means "beloved of God." That's you! That's me! But his Gospel was written for specific "Beloveds of God." It won't speak to you unless you fit into some of the following categories. Check as many as possible!

1. Poor, in need of hope
2. Sinner, in need of forgiveness
3. Lonely, in need of a friend
4. Depressed, in need of Good News
5. Sad, in need of joy
6. Female, in need of affirmation
7. Struggling, on a faith pilgrimage
8. Searching, seeking God
9. Have the blahs, in need of a song
10. Bogged down, in need of a vision

Score:

6 or less: Gospel doesn't apply. It's only for struggling Christians.

7 to 8: Keep reading. The cure is as close as your Bible.

9 to 10: Luke must have had you in mind when he wrote. This is your personal Gospel!

Two Births

Notice the actors who appear on the stage in the first act of this drama. (It is set in two scenes, the birth of John the Baptist, and the birth of the Messiah,

THE HEART OF LUKE'S GOSPEL: 4:16-21

Jesus came to Nazareth where he had grown up, and went according to his custom into the synagogue on the sabbath day. He stood up to read and was handed a scroll of the prophet Isaiah. He unrolled the scroll and found the passage where it was written:

The Spirit of the Lord is upon me,
because he has anointed me
to bring glad tidings to the poor.
He has sent me to proclaim liberty to captives
and recovery of sight to the blind,
to let the oppressed go free,

Rolling up the scroll, he handed it back to the attendant and sat down, and the eyes of all in the synagogue looked intently at him. He said to them, "Today this scripture passage is fulfilled in your hearing."

Jesus.) Zechariah, elderly, with no heir and no hope of one, a priest, one among so many that this might have been the only time in his entire life that he got to serve; Elizabeth his wife, elderly and, worse, barren, which is perceived as a curse from God. To their neighbors they seem the most unfortunate of people. But God has other plans. He calls them out of retirement, unlikely as they are, to be a major channel of his blessings. They will not only have the blessing they had almost despaired of - a child, but this child will play a pivotal role in the plan of salvation. His name, John, says it all: "God is gracious." The God of surprises is at it again. But this is only scene one.

In scene two a teen-age girl, betrothed but unmarried, is told by God's messenger that she will conceive a child to be called the "Son of the Most High." Only because she has already conceived God in her heart in faith can she now say yes to conceiving him in her womb. Anyone else would be dismayed. Mary goes off on a ninety-mile journey to sing of the pregnancy to her cousin, Elizabeth, proclaiming the theme of the whole Gospel: "My soul proclaims the greatness of the Lord; my spirit rejoices in God my savior.... God has thrown down the rulers from their thrones, but lifted up the lowly." The God of surprises exalts, lifts up the lowly, the poor, the unlikely.

Zechariah continues singing Mary's song in his Benedictus at the birth of the Baptist (Luke 1:68-79), and the angels pick up the tune in Bethlehem as they announce the joyful news of the Messiah's birth to...the religious authorities? No! To the political rulers on their thrones? No! To the sophisticates of Jerusalem? No! To the

poor, lowly, despised, distrusted shepherds? Incredibly, yes! "Glory to God in the highest and peace to God's people on earth" (Luke 2:14). As St. Augustine said, "The Glory of God is ourselves fully alive." That's worth singing about and that's why Luke's Gospel is so full of joy and song. It is the story of Jesus, God with us, touching, healing, blessing, consoling, forgiving, making us fully alive.

For Jesus, the greatest miracle is the power of his Word that awakens slumbering faith and brings about conversion of heart, inviting us into the Reign of God.

*"Poor creature
though I be, I am
the hand and foot of
Christ...for Deity is
become inseparably
one" (Symeon, the New
Theologian).*

Job Description

Such is the job description Jesus adopts for himself in chapter 4. In the temptations, he has already rejected the dole-dispensing, conquering, razzle-dazzle job description of the messianic hope of his time. He is the Messiah, but on his own terms, as he tells neighbor and kin in the synagogue of Nazareth when he quotes from another song, Isaiah's servant song:

> `The Spirit of the Lord is upon me, because he has anointed me to bring glad tidings to the poor. He has sent me to proclaim liberty to captives and recovery of sight to the blind, to let the oppressed go free, and to proclaim a year acceptable to the Lord.'
> Rolling up the scroll he handed it back to the attendant and sat down, and the eyes of all in the synagogue looked intently at him. He said to them, 'Today this scripture passage is fulfilled in your hearing' (4:18-21; Isaiah 61:1-2).

From the very beginning God's plan and human expectations are on a collision course. Jesus' contemporaries knew how God should act: The poor, captive, blind and oppressed were that way because they deserved it as a punishment from God. They also labeled Jesus as misguided, accusing him of blasphemously upsetting their perception of an avenging God. He had even omitted half of the last line from the quote: "and a day of vindication by our God." That was the line they really liked.

They were also enraged that he identified himself as a prophet without honor in his own country. If they had misread the role of the Messiah, they had also forgotten the role of the prophet. They wanted someone who would point the finger at God's enemies. True enough, but they could not imagine what was so eloquently said by a modern cartoon character: "We have met the enemy, and they are us."

A prophet is someone who comforts the afflicted and afflicts the comfortable. They were too comfortable in their pre-conceived notions of how God should act and how the Messiah should function, and so they were unable to accept Jesus. They had made God in their image and likeness. But "'My thoughts are not your thoughts nor are your ways my ways,' says the Lord" (Isaiah 55:8). So Jesus left them and went to "the hungry and lowly," as his mother had sung. He went to those who were so far down, they had no place to look but up, and departed from those who had exalted their own expectations to the level of God's will.

In his editing and arranging of the stories that have come down to him from Mark, from the "Q" catechetical source, and from the private tales of his own community, Luke is a master of contrast. He has just shown that Jesus "came to his own and his own received him not" (John 1:11). He immediately shows that even a demon has more perception, recognition and insight than Jesus' listeners: "I know who you are - the Holy One of God" (Luke 4:34).

Calling Commoners

Fortified with his job description, Jesus now goes forth to do his job. He doesn't head for the smug, complacent, self-righteous religious professionals. "Those who are `healthy' do not need a physician. I have not come to call the `righteous' to repentance, but sinners" (Mark 2:17). He starts with a doubting, self-admitted sinner named Simon (later on, Peter) whose theological education

"He said to them: 'Come after me, and I will make you fishers of others'" (Matthew 4:19).

began in his fishing boat. Before the fisherman knows what is happening, he, not the fish, is hooked (5:1-11).

Jesus adds insult to injury by calling a thieving, cheating tax collector. Like all tax collectors of the time, this man was a traitor, collaborating with the Romans, the very enemies the Messiah was supposed to liberate them from. Lowly? You couldn't get much lower! But these are the new wine skins into which Jesus will pour his new wine (5:37).

Luke in chapter 6 portrays Jesus outlining his agenda. Matthew has provided a mountain as a setting, but Luke continues his theme of lowliness even geographically. For him it is the Sermon on the Plain.

Jesus' contemporaries thought they were blessed by God when they were rich, filled, amused and affirmed. The God of surprises strikes again. Jesus says that the poor, hungry, weeping and misunderstood are the blessed, the special friends of God. The rest of the message, like the rest of the Gospel, is a call to do the unexpected, to go beyond what would be the merely

human response: "Love your enemies, turn the other cheek, give more than is requested or even demanded, lend with no expectation of return, stop judging" (cf. Matthew 5-6), and on it goes. How impractical Jesus is. How beyond reach his Gospel demands are. But Jesus knew what he was doing. If we reach for something and can't get it, we'll ask for help. That's prayer. Just what the Gospel ordered.

Later on (chapter 18), Jesus illustrates his point of view with the parable of the Pharisee and the tax collector. For the former, religion is obeying laws, and the Pharisee thinks he can do that very well by himself, thank you. With his "do it yourself sanctity kit," his trip to the temple results not in prayer, but in a progress report. The tax collector, on the other hand, knows he has fallen short of the goal. That's the biblical meaning of sin. He cries out for help. That's prayer. The gospel demands are unrealistic and impossible without it.

Throughout Luke's Gospel Jesus has no kind word for the Pharisees, the professional religious who are missing the point and don't know it. They are self-made men who have no one to blame but themselves. Jesus sticks with the ones they despise as being irreligious.

Insider Praying

Prayer is a major theme for Luke. The closed-mindedness of the "pious" and the openness of the lowly give rise to Jesus' own prayer: "I give you praise, Father, Lord of heaven and earth, for although you have hidden these things from the wise and learned, you have revealed them to the childlike" (10:21). In chapter 11 we find Jesus' central teaching on prayer. Notice that when he responds to his friends' request to be taught how to pray, he says not "Our Father," the formal title found in Matthew, but "Father" which better reflects the Aramaic language that Jesus used. He actually said "Abba," which means "Daddy." Never before, even in all of the one hundred and fifty prayers of the Old Testament that we call psalms, had God been addressed with such intimacy. Neither Abraham, Moses nor David had dared to do it. But Jesus had brought his disciples into such a close relationship with his Father that he tells them to call God, Abba, Daddy.

The next section (11:5-13) at first looks just like some good advice about perseverance in prayer. And it is that, but look what Luke does with the last line. Matthew's statement that God "will give good things to those who ask" (7:11), becomes in Luke, "[God] will give the Holy Spirit to those who ask" (11:13). For Luke, writing fifty years after Pentecost, the Holy Spirit is the sum of all good gifts, the answer to every prayer. As Paul, whom Luke probably knew, writes to the Romans: "For those who are led by the Spirit of God are the children of God.... You received a spirit of adoption by which

MIRACLES

Jesus never tried to prove himself. He never worked a miracle "to prove" who he was. In the last desperate hour on the cross he refused to respond to their challenge: "Let the Messiah, the King of Israel, come down now from the cross that we may see and believe" (Mark 15:32). Even if he had, it would not have worked. Even miracles were ineffective with spiritually blind unbelievers.

Earlier in his ministry when a sign from heaven was demanded of him he replied:

> This generation is an evil generation; it seeks a sign, but no sign will be given it, except the sign of Jonah. Just as Jonah became a sign to the Ninevites, so will the Son of Man be to this generation.... At the judgment, the people of Nineveh will arise with this generation and condemn it, because at the preaching of Jonah they repented, and there is something greater than Jonah here (Luke 11:29-32).

For Jesus, the greatest miracle is the power of his Word that awakens slumbering faith and brings about conversion of hearts, inviting us into the Reign of God. Notice how often he doesn't even attribute a miraculous cure to himself, but says: "Your faith has saved you."

Walking on water, multiplying loaves, healing, raising the dead, all the marvelous miracles that he worked are all signs of the breaking in of the Reign of God in his person. To the bystander standing outside they are amazing. To the believer they are beckoning signs: "The Reign of God is here." Get a move on!

The Gospel is the story of Jesus, God with us, touching healing, blessing, consoling, forgiving, making us fully alive.

we cry, 'Abba, Father'" (8:14).

Through parable and invitation Jesus continues to bring the most unlikely, "lowly" candidates to a new life in the Father: his Daddy and theirs. "No one knows the Father except the Son and anyone to whom the Son wishes to reveal him" (10:22). Notice how often this life with God through discipleship with the Son in the power of the Spirit is expressed in the context of a meal. It is a very human time for sharing. Even the English word "companion" comes from the Latin "cum panis," i.e., together with bread.

Breaking Barriers

It is while sharing the hospitality of his companions Martha and Mary that he does the most incredible, unheard-of thing, never before done in the history of God's people. He opens up discipleship to women. It is the better part that Mary has chosen which will not be taken away from her. Martha is not wrong. She's just missing the boat (11:38-42).

In Jericho, Zachaeus, the local turn-coat tax collector whom everyone looks down on, is looked up to by Jesus; and the occasion is celebrated when he becomes Zachaeus' house guest. With both of these stories, unique to him, Luke is at pains to point out something that could easily be missed. While some disciples are told to sell all and give to the poor, Martha and Mary are not told to put their house on the market; and Jesus is satisfied with Zachaeus' giving half of his possessions to the poor. Clearly, Martha and Mary of Bethany and Zachaeus of Jericho are not depicted as half-hearted disciples. With Jesus, the important thing is not merely what they give to others, but that they give themselves to him. There are as many manifestations of discipleship as there are disciples.

Luke's framework and over-arching motif for the stories about Jesus that have come down to him is one of pilgrimage. Time and time again as Jesus goes through Galilee doing good, it is mentioned that his goal is the holy city, Jerusalem, the place of God's revelation. Even as an infant presented there, or an adolescent lost there, Jesus' home is his Father's home. In chapter 2 he is already saying to his mother: "Why were you looking for me? Did you not know that I must be in my

"...that terrible tree, which is the death of God and the life of man" (GK Chesterton).

Father's house?" Even while he is exalting the lowly, there is a homesickness that tugs at him. All of this is to let us know that his fate there, his passion and death, was not a senseless tragedy. This was part of the job description he had embraced at the beginning, the role of the suffering servant:

> While we thought of him as stricken, as one smitten by God and afflicted....
> Upon him was the chastisement that makes us whole.
> By his stripes we were healed....
> Oppressed and condemned he was taken away and who would have thought any more of his destiny?...
> Because of his affliction, he shall see light in the fullness of days (Isaiah 53).

While the whole Gospel is addressed to Luke's community in the year 80, the last chapter is especially so. It is addressed to us as well and to all who unrealistically yearn to go back and talk to Jesus and be with him. It is possible to touch and be touched by Jesus, but not by going back. Rather it is by

hearing his Word, as the disciples on the road to Emmaus learned: "Were not our hearts burning within us while he spoke to us on the way, and opened the Scriptures to us?" (Luke 24:32). He is still with us in his Word. "Then the two recounted what had taken place on the way, and how they recognized him in the Breaking of the Bread" (Luke 24:35). He is still with us in the Eucharist.

The Gospel ends with the Ascension. He had to go, but he found a way to stay: Word and Sacrament. But Luke's Gospel is not over, because the work of Jesus is not over. Jesus is also to be found in his community, the Church. The other half of Luke's Gospel, called the Acts of the Apostles, will tell us about that.

4

ACTS OF
THE APOSTLES

Luke would not have been too happy with what a later Church did to this second part of his work. Instead of calling it the Gospel of Luke, Part Two, as he intended, they gave it a new and misleading name. Worse, in the official list of sacred books they inserted John between the first and second parts of Luke's Gospel. Thus the impression was given that what is now called "Acts" is different from the four Gospels in literary form, intent, purpose and leading characters involved.

Spirited Partnership

Chapter 2 lets us know why "Acts of the Apostles" is a misnomer. What it really reveals is the Acts of the Holy Spirit at work within the apostles. They are no more able to act without the Spirit now than they were able to act without Jesus in the first part of Luke's work.

Luke composes a dramatic setting for the sending of the Spirit. John 20:22 states that it took place on Easter Sunday. For Luke that is too much to comprehend all at once. He separates the events by 50 days to coincide with the Jewish feast of Pentecost. If Jesus' passing over from death to life gave Passover a new meaning, then the experience of life in the Spirit can give the next Jewish feast, Pentecost, a new meaning.

Seven weeks after Passover the wheat harvest was gathered. This was the concrete proof that God had lived up to the promise of giving the people the land. In their turn they wanted to signify that they would fulfill their promise and obey God's will. From the flour of the new grain they fashioned two loaves, symbolic of the tablets of the Law, the guide of their life. Since Jesus fulfilled the Law and replaced it with the gift of the Holy Spirit, what better feast on which to celebrate that than the feast of Pentecost? "If you are guided by the Spirit, you are not under the Law" (Galatians 5:18).

That gift of the Spirit so profoundly affected the disciples that the bystanders thought they were drunk. Far from it. They had been transformed from cowering, timid, hide-aways to excited enthusiasts. Enthusiasm comes from a Greek word meaning "in God" (en theos). That's what they were excited

Not so. If the first part is not biography, but an invitation to discipleship, then neither is the second part to be considered an historical treatise on early Christianity. It too is a call to discipleship with the risen Lord. The characters have not changed. The Gospel is centered on Jesus, the Messiah, bearer of the Spirit. Acts focuses on Jesus the risen Lord, the bestower of the Spirit present in his Church. If there is a change, it is in the goal of the pilgrimage. In the Gospel, it is Jerusalem, the privileged place of God's encounter with his people and of his revelation to them. In Acts, the goal is Rome, capital of the conqueror of the world, which itself will now be conquered by the Lord Jesus.

about. They were in God by the power of the Holy Spirit and Jesus was Lord of their lives. He was in charge. They didn't have to be nervous Nelly's about their own weaknesses and limitations any more. Paul put it in a nutshell: "You cannot proclaim that Jesus is Lord unless the Holy Spirit is with you" (cf. 1 Corinthians 12:3). Now, confronted with any danger, crisis or disappointment, they just needed to remind themselves "Jesus is Lord," and they knew they were not alone. They knew who was in charge.

Now they could go out and take on the world, and indeed the empire. It belonged to Jesus anyway. He was Lord.

Change of Lifestyle

By their lifestyle they showed who was in charge:

> They devoted themselves to the apostles' instruction and the communal life, to the breaking of bread and the prayers. A reverent fear overtook them all, for many wonders and signs were performed by the apostles. Those who believed shared

"Jesus Christ became what we are that he might make us what he is" (Athanasius of Alexandria).

all things in common; they would sell their property and goods, dividing everything on the basis of each one's need. They went to the temple area together every day, while in their homes they broke bread. With exultant and sincere hearts they took their meals in common, praising God and winning the approval of all the people. Day by day the Lord added to their number those who were being saved (Acts 2:42-47).

Thus the early Jerusalem community became the model of every Christian community. Conscious of Jesus in their midst, united in faith, supported in love, strengthened by the Word, rejoicing in the Breaking of the Bread which made them one, their life was already a living proclamation of the Gospel.

But good news has to be shared. The gift of the Spirit gave them an irresistible compulsion to spread it. Of course, the establishment didn't take kindly to this new movement. It was a prophetic movement, and one of the roles of a prophet is to remind the establishment what it was established for. By the fact that they preached Jesus, and not the Law, as the Way, they antagonized the professional custodians of the Law. Dragged before the religious court (Sanhedrin), they were forbidden to preach. Their reply? "It is impossible for us not to speak about what we have seen and heard" (Acts 4:20).

Tension Inside and Out

Stephen, accused of blasphemy, lost his life as a "martyr," which means "witness." Thus developed the saying "the blood of martyrs is the seed of the Church." The despised and lowly Samaritans came flocking to the Gospel; the ambassador of the Queen of Ethiopia embraced it, and - the God of surprises is at work again - Saul, rab-

FAITH

The Gospels are an invitation to faith; Jesus demands faith and praises it. The Acts of the Apostles present the demand to faith in the risen Jesus continuing his mission through the Holy Spirit.

Jesus' parables presuppose faith and his miracles are ineffective, if not impossible, without it. "He did not (Mark 6:5 "could not") work many mighty deeds there, because of their lack of faith" (Matthew 13:58).

What is this FAITH? Is it the ability at Sunday worship to recite the creed without skipping a dogma? Hardly, since there were no creeds in Jesus' time. It is what we refer to in the Mass when, in the first eucharistic prayer, we speak of "Abraham, our father in faith." The root of the word in Hebrew, the language of Abraham, is

Amunah, the same root for the word "Amen." It means to be firm, well established, with a sure foundation, as in Jesus' parable of building one's house on a solid foundation (Matthew 7:24).

Faith is not a formula. It is a center of gravity. It is a total response to a life under the Reign of God. It is the answer to the question: "What makes you tick?"

ble-rouser, accuser, and instigator of the persecution, becomes, in a flash of grace-filled light, Paul the apostle of the Gentiles.

His dramatic experience on the road to Damascus was his introduction to Jesus, who forcefully told him that what he did to the Church he did to Jesus himself. Paul never forgot that the Church is the Body of Christ, not just a society united in allegiance to him. Paul's conversion from a religion based on laws, as he perceived it, to one centered on the person of Jesus Christ, dismayed not only his previous colleagues, but also caused serious tension in the newfound community into which he had been incorporated. The Jewish Christians of Jerusalem were reluctant to let go of their inheritance of laws and practices.

After Paul's first missionary journey to the Gentiles, he arrived at Jerusalem looking for affirmation for his success. "But some from the party of the Pharisees who had become believers stood up and said: 'It is necessary to circumcise them and direct them to observe the Mosaic Law'" (Acts 15:1). The family of Christ was split by a domestic quarrel which threatened to divide the Body of Christ, for Paul's stand was quite the opposite. He minced no words: "Beware of the dogs. Beware of the evil workers. Beware of the mutilation (circumcision!!).... I consider everything as a loss because of the supreme good of knowing Christ Jesus my Lord" (Philippians 3:2,8).

James, the head of the Jerusalem Church, settled the matter by reducing the demands to the least common denominator, and that did not include circumcision. The Gentiles were to have nothing to do with idols, which was logical if Jesus was Lord. They were to

avoid illicit sexual unions, the very thing Jesus had taught. Finally, they were to avoid blood, sacred to the Jews, for whom blood was life and life was the domain of God.

The dispute, now out in the open, was not settled by a letter, however. The role of law in relation to Gospel haunted the Church right to the end of Paul's life and still does in our day.

From chapter 15 (the Council of Jerusalem) right to the end of chapter 28, Luke's preoccupation is to show the spread of the Gospel to the very ends of the empire. But the work of the Holy Spirit finds its fulfillment when Paul arrives at Rome, the heart of the empire. Even under house arrest, "With complete assurance and without hindrance he proclaimed the Reign of God and taught about the Lord Jesus Christ" (Acts 28:30). Jerusalem and Rome have been conquered by Jesus who is Lord.

Conscious of Jesus in their midst, united in faith, supported in love, strengthened by the Word, rejoicing in the Breaking of the Bread which made them one, the life of the early Christians was already a living proclamation of the Gospel.

5

THE GOSPEL ACCORDING TO JOHN

The Evangelist "On Eagles Wings"

One of the thrilling things about a
pilgrimage to the Holy Land is a
visit to a tell to see the archaeologists at work.
A tell is an artificial mound built up of the
remnants and debris of all the civilizations that
have occupied the area over centuries. The
experts peel off layer after layer revealing
culture, values, and life style of the ancient
peoples at each level. For instance, at Tell es
Sultan or ancient Jericho, the oldest
continuously inhabited city in the world, the
remains of at least thirty levels of habitation
have been revealed.

Although each of the Gospels is like a tell revealing the three levels - Jesus, the Church, and the Evangelist - John's Gospel contains many more. Not completed until the end of the first century, it reveals level upon level of the community's experience of the risen Lord and his meaning in their lives. At one point in the evolution and development of the Gospel, the upper room scene must have ended at 14:31 when Jesus says "Get up, let us go." It is not until three chapters later that they do; those three chapters are filled with other traditions and fruits of meditation within the Johannine community.

The goal of every archaeologist is to get to the bottom of things, the earliest level of habitation. In this tell-Gospel, we get to the bottom of things, and that is Jesus. But it is the Jesus perceived through several generations of faith. To see him we have to borrow the rose-tinted glasses of the faith and prayer that characterized the community to which the disciples first preached the risen Lord.

THE HEART OF JOHN'S GOSPEL

Getting to the heart of John's Gospel, a Gospel filled with layers of mystery, theology and spirituality, requires prayerful insight. The core is found in the prologue which has rightly been called an overture to a symphony. Musically, an overture telescopes all of those themes that will be elaborated and expanded in the rest of the work. The prologue is a work of art, a poem in a Semitic form that may not be familiar to us, except in the psalms. Its essence is not in rhyme or meter, but in parallelism. The second line repeats, paraphrases, echoes, or expands upon the first.

John employed a special variety of this form called "enveloping parallelism": The first line corresponds to the last, and the second line to the next to the last, until it envelopes the central theme that has no parallel. In the prologue it is: "To those who did accept him he gave the power to become children of God, to those who believe in his name, who were born not by natural generation nor by human choice nor by a person's decision but of God."

Prologue (Summary of Johannine Thought) John 1:1-18

A. (vs. 1-2) The Word with God   A. (vs. 18) The Son in the Father
B. (vs. 3) His role in Creation   B. (vs. 17) Role of re-creation
C. (vs. 4-5) Gift to us   C. (vs. 16) Gift to us
D. (vs. 6-8) Witness of John   D. (vs. 15) Witness of John
E. (vs. 9-11) Coming of the Word   E. (vs. 14) The Incarnation
         F. (vs. 12-13) God-become-human gives humans power
                    to become the children of God

Mastering Meaning

Surprisingly, this Gospel doesn't share with us very many of the facts and statistics of Jesus' life. It isn't kidding when it concludes: "There are also many other things that Jesus did" (21:25). But what John and his community do tell us, they tell us in a way that shows great depth and theological and spiritual penetration into the life and teachings of Jesus. That is why the original evangelist has been nick-named John the "Theologian," symbolized as a soaring eagle with a magnificent perspective of what's going on down below. Some people only ask "What happened?" and they get the bare facts and statistics. John and his community stand with those who go further and ask, "What's going on?" What they discover is the profound mystery of the events. Notice how the evangelists start their Gospels: Mark in Galilee, Matthew in the past genealogy of Jesus' ancestors, and Luke in the temple. John leaves them all behind when he soars to the heavens, indeed, into eternity: "In the beginning was the Word, and the Word was with God and the Word was God" (John 1:1). Wow! But by the first three words he also plunges us back into time, "in the beginning." They are to evoke in us the memory of the first three words of the creation account in Genesis. He wants to get us "psyched up" for the rest of the story. It announces a new creation. In the first account the human race is created, but in this new one the children of God are created. "To those who did accept him he gave the power to become the children of God" (1:12).

Notice that the text doesn't say he "made" them children of God, but gave them the "power of becoming." It is this

The tomb of Christ within the Church of the Holy Sepulchre in Jerusalem.

"becoming" and the problems attendant upon it to which the Gospel addresses itself.

Critical Times

One of the problems was that they were still trying to find out what was the difference between a Christian and a Jew. The Jews solved the problem for them by throwing them out of the synagogue. Like a young eagle being thrown out of the nest by its parent, they squawked at first; but it was one of the best things that ever happened to them. Chapter 9 is a good reflection of this critical time in the community of John in 90 A.D.: "They were afraid of the Jews, who had already agreed that if anyone acknowledged him as Messiah he would be expelled from the

Eucharist is Jesus' gift of himself to us; his legacy is life, "the fullness of which we have all had a share, love overflowing upon love" (John 1:16).

synagogue" (9:22). The prediction of Jesus in 16:2 is really a reflection of the community situation in the year 90. "They will expel you from the synagogues; in fact, the hour is coming when everyone who kills you will think he is offering worship to God." Dark days indeed for the young Church, but days that began to help them perceive the light of their own call in Christ. Unfortunately, that left them with a negative feeling for some of the Jews which later generations misinterpreted and twisted into anti-semitism.

Another problem which John's community had to face was the delay of the Second Coming and, therefore, of the last judgment. By 90 A.D., it had not occurred, and a lot of them were getting comfortable and complacent. John startled them by saying that the last judgment takes place every day. "The judgment of condemnation is this: The

light came into the world, but people loved darkness rather than light because their deeds were wicked" (3:19).

Trial and Error

So, for John, trial, judgment and verdict are not something that happens to Jesus at the end of his life. "He (the Father) gave him (the Son) power to exercise judgment, because he is the Son of Man" (5:27). It is up to Jesus to call the witnesses, and he does: the Baptist, his own works, the Father, the Scriptures and Moses himself (5:31-46). He even appoints a defense lawyer (Advocate) for his followers: the Holy Spirit (14:15ff). To make his point about who is in charge of the real trial, in his Greek text, John makes it ambiguous about who sat on the judgment seat, Jesus or Pilate (19:13)!

If the trial reveals that Jesus has enemies, the Gospel also reveals that his worst enemies are smug, self-complacent, mediocre Christians, who identify being religious with going to church or receiving the sacraments. For this reason, John, the most sacramental of the Gospels with its mention of the signs of water, light, bread and wine, omits the institution of the Eucharist, which has come to be taken for granted and to be misunderstood by the community. At the last supper it is replaced by the washing of the feet. They had come to view the Eucharist as Jesus' gift of himself to them. They failed to see it as a challenge to give themselves to each other. "I have given you a model to follow, so that as I have done for you, you should also do" (13:15). Of all the inspired words of God, perhaps the most inspiring are the following three chapters, and they have been aptly called a homily on the

John's followers were satisfied that the empty tomb and the appearances pointed to only one possible conclusion: "The light shines in the darkness and the darkness has not overcome it" (John 1:5).

Eucharist summed up so beautifully in chapter 15: "Love one another as I love you. No one has greater love than this, to lay down one's life for one's friends" (15:12).

Book of Glory

The first part of the Gospel is concerned with the signs that Jesus performed, challenging the believer to deeper faith. The second part (chapter 13 ff) has been called the Book of Glory. Jesus walks majestically through its pages to the cross as to a throne. It is Jesus' "hour" that he had alluded to at the first of his signs, the wedding feast at Cana. In John, there is no "agony" in the garden, as if Jesus were overwhelmed and powerless. He confronts those coming to arrest him with the proclamation made to Moses in the burning bush. He is "I Am." In the normal reaction of those who have just met their God, "They turned away and fell to the ground" (18:5).

For John's community, the Gospel is not a tragedy with a happy ending. Jesus has been Lord and in control from the very beginning until the end: "This is why the Father loves me, because I lay down my life in order to take it up again. No one takes it from me, but I lay it down on my own" (10:17).

This Gospel of unbounded love presents one more figure that personifies it. She is the Woman (Eve was the Woman of the first creation) who is also mother (Eve's name means `mother of all the living'). John doesn't

tell us her name, but in writing of Mary, he tells us what she does. She is "Woman" and "Mother." She is the intercessor who gets him to anticipate his "hour" in the first of his signs at Cana, changing water to wine. She is Jesus' gift to John, his community and ourselves at the fulfillment of his hour (19:26).

But the generosity of our Lord is not over. John doesn't even mention that Jesus died. "And bowing his head, he handed over the Spirit" (19:30). He promised not to leave us orphans and he didn't.

On the "third day" when the risen Lord comes to his community to breathe upon them the Holy Spirit, the promise of the prologue is gloriously fulfilled in them and in us:

> The Word became flesh and made his dwelling among us. And we have seen his glory: the glory of an only son coming from the Father, filled with enduring love. Of his fullness we have all had a share, love overflowing upon love (John 1:14, 16).

Yet the "hour" of Jesus is not primarily determined by a clock, but by his passover through death to resurrection. There would have been no Gospel without it, for there would have been no good news. The hour is when he becomes Lord of death and thus the Lord of glory.

Those people who say they can accept Jesus as a good teacher, but not as risen Lord or Son of God, do violence to the Gospels. As Paul wrote: "If Christ has not been raised, then empty is our preaching; empty, too, is your faith.... If Christ has not been raised, your faith is vain; you are still in your sins" (1 Corinthians 15:14). Jesus' legacy is not a high level of ethical teaching. It is life, that "fullness of which we have all had a share, love overflowing upon love" (John 1:16).

The Empty Tomb

No one in the Gospels ever claimed to have witnessed the resurrection, except in a slanderous story about soldiers stealing the body (Matthew 28:11-15). The community never tried to counteract such a rumor by making up stories about the resurrection, which they could easily have done. They were satisfied that the empty tomb and the appearances pointed to only one possible conclusion: "The light shines in the darkness and the darkness has not overcome it" (John 1:5). Jesus, their Lord and Messiah, was truly risen.

His resurrection, however, should never be confused with resuscitation. What happened to Lazarus and what happened to Jesus are two entirely different experiences. Jesus raised Lazarus to life. He came back to the very same natural, normal life that he had left. Jesus did not. In his "hour" he passed over from time into eternity, into a state transformed, glorified and life-giving.

The risen Jesus was the same, yet he was different. Magdalene thought he was the gardener. On the road to Emmaus, the two disciples did not recognize him until he broke bread with them. In the upper room, even with the door closed, he came and was present to them. He was their risen Lord.

And yet he is the same Jesus. John tells us that on the shore of the Sea of Galilee Jesus cooked breakfast for them. In Matthew's Gospel they took hold of his feet and worshipped him. Back in John's Gospel he tells doubting Thomas to touch him. He is real, no figment of their imagination or phantasm. Yet he is different, the glorified and risen Lord.

The message of all four Gospels, as well as of Paul, is faith in the Lord Jesus who conquered sin and death. No one saw the resurrection, but Jesus' words to Thomas were meant for us: "Blessed are those who have not seen and yet believe" (John 20:29).

John's community, sixty years after the resurrection, had not witnessed the event, but they had seen the risen Lord in the community in which they lived. They were living witnesses of Paul's words:

> May the God of our Lord Jesus Christ, the Father of glory, grant you a spirit of wisdom and insight to know God clearly. May God enlighten your innermost vision that you may know the great hope to which God has called you, the wealth of God's glorious heritage to be distributed among the members of the Church,

and the immeasurable scope of God's power in us who believe. It is like the strength God showed in raising Christ from the dead (Ephesians 1:17-20).

"The beauty of the world is Christ's tender smile for us coming through matter." (Simone Weil)

NEW TESTAMENT EPISTLES INTRODUCTION

When we think of the New Testament we think mostly of Gospels. But much of the New Testament consists of letters mostly written before anyone thought of writing a Gospel. They were written for an adolescent Church going through an identity crisis. Imagine writing to a young daughter away from home for the first time, perhaps at college. She is facing new situations, challenges to her maturity. When you write to advise her, drawing from your own wisdom, experience, successes and failures, you are doing exactly what Paul did. So did Peter, James, John, Jude and all the New Testament writers.

Since their letters were offering solutions and answers, we must read between the lines to find out what the problems and the questions were. We'll likely find out that they were the same problems that the growing, struggling community has today. That's why the solutions and answers, called New Testament epistles, are still valid. As the Word of God, they were not preserved to satisfy our curiosity about the struggles of the adolescent Church of the first century. They still speak to us adolescent, immature, growing Christians of the twentieth century. They still beckon us to maturity in Christ.

PAUL

Paul of Tarsus (in present day Turkey) wrote more of the New Testament than any other author.

Born and educated outside of the center of Judaism (Jerusalem), Paul still aligned himself with a strain of the strictest, law-observant and at times fanatical sect of the Jews: the Pharisees. At the same time, his upbringing had given him an outlook that benefitted from Greek learning and Roman power and administrative efficiency. His great boast was that he possessed one of the most coveted badges of prestige at that time: Roman citizenship. His religious and civil heritages were as dear to him as life.

He first emerges on the pages of the New Testament as a biased, intolerant bigot. His cherished and unyielding religious beliefs were being challenged by a Jewish group called "the Way." They proclaimed that the way to God was no longer by strict following of the 613 precepts, rules and regulations of the law, but by following Jesus their risen Lord who is the Way, the Truth and the Life. For Paul this was blasphemy and had to be punished with death. In Jerusalem he presided over the stoning to death of Stephen. Resolved to eradicate this heresy, he set out to destroy the young Church in Damascus (Syria).

But the eyes that gleamed with hatred soon beheld his very enemy. He encountered Jesus in a profound experience that changed his life and the course of history. The Lord had one question for him: "Why are you persecuting me?" (Acts 9:4). Confused, because he had no argument with this stranger whose encounter had thrown him to the ground and left him blind, he asked his identity. "I am Jesus, whom you are persecuting." Dramatically Paul came to realize that the way we treat others is the way we treat Jesus. This is called the conversion of Paul.

All the unbridled anger that Paul had previously unleashed against the "Way" was transformed into a burning compulsion to spread the "Good News." When you read the Acts of the Apostles, about his travels, and

the letters that he wrote to so many Churches, just imagine what Paul could have accomplished with an air travel credit card and a word processor!

The example of Paul can be discouraging for us Christians who plod along in the struggle to live the Gospel and proclaim the faith. He seems to have had it made with his instantaneous and dramatic conversion to Jesus. Not so. Twenty years later he could still write: "It is not that I...have already achieved perfect maturity, but I continue my pursuit in the hope that I may possess it, since I indeed have been taken possession of by Christ Jesus" (Philippians 3:12). Hand in hand with him, we continue our pursuit.

Paul, in his own words:

> If anyone else thinks he can be confident in flesh, all the more can I. Circumcised on the eighth day, of the race of Israel, of the tribe of Benjamin, a Hebrew of Hebrew parentage, in observance of the law a Pharisee, in zeal I persecuted the Church, in righteousness based on the law I was blameless.
>
> But whatever gains I had, these I have come to consider a loss because of Christ. More than that, I even consider everything as a loss because of the supreme good of knowing Christ Jesus my Lord. For his sake I have accepted the loss of all things and I consider them so much rubbish, that I may gain Christ and be found in him, not having any righteousness of my own based on the law but that which comes through faith in Christ, the righteousness from God, depending on faith to know him and the power of his resurrection and the sharing of his sufferings by being conformed to his death (Philippians 3:4b-10).

Definitions:

FLESH: For Paul this is the merely human, weak, powerless person, without God, without Christ, without hope, the pathetic self-made individual.

RIGHTEOUSNESS: (also called Justification) This is the right relationship with God, his gift of grace which makes us his sons and daughters. It has other synonyms: salvation, redemption, new creation, etc.

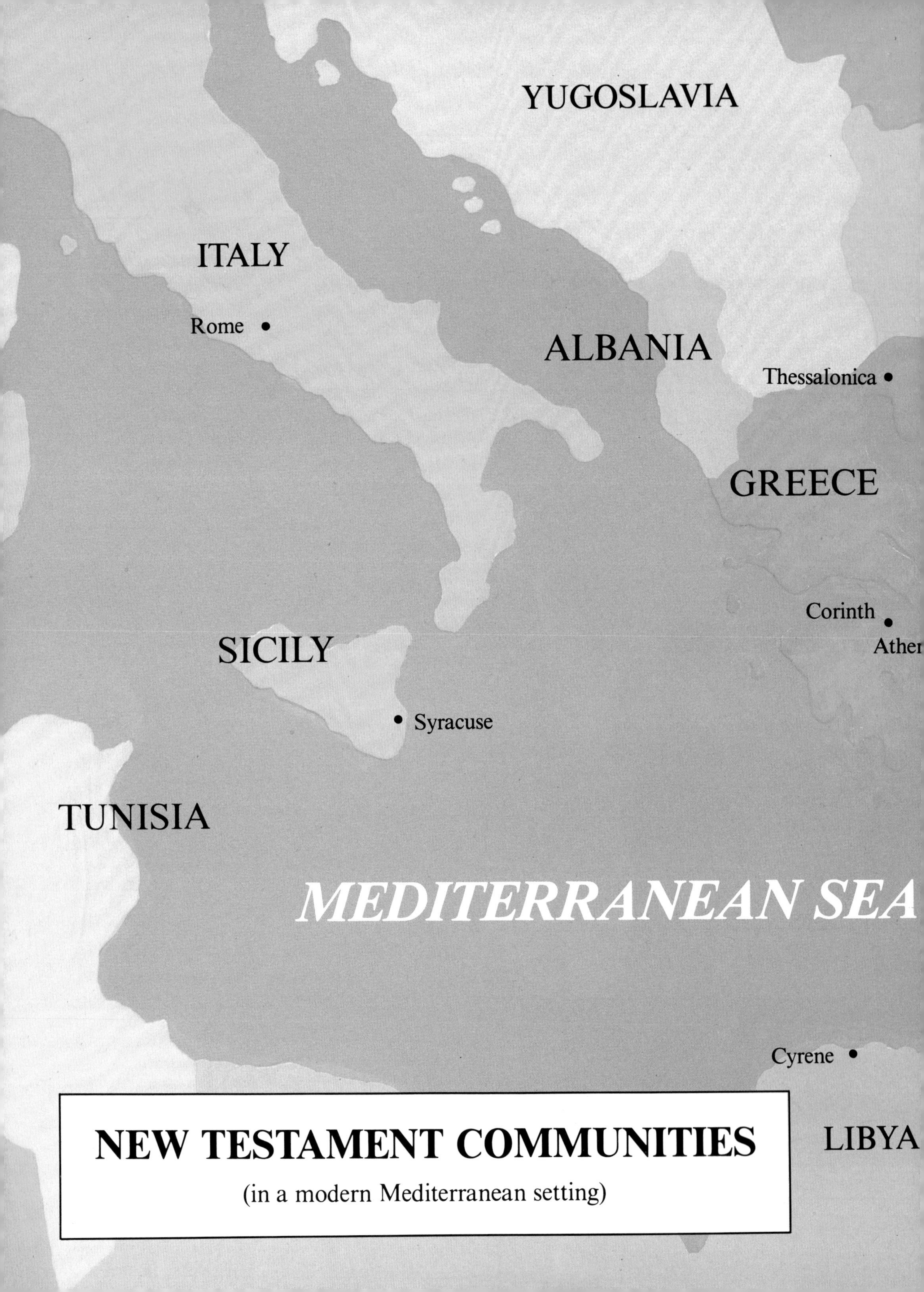

YUGOSLAVIA

ITALY

Rome •

ALBANIA

Thessalonica •

GREECE

Corinth •
Ather

SICILY

• Syracuse

TUNISIA

MEDITERRANEAN SEA

Cyrene •

NEW TESTAMENT COMMUNITIES

LIBYA

(in a modern Mediterranean setting)

ROMANIA

BULGARIA

BLACK SEA

Philippi

GALATIA

TURKEY

• Ephesus   • Colossae

Tarsus •

• Antioch

PATMOS

SYRIA

CRETE   CYPRUS

LEBANON

Damascus •

ISRAEL   JORDAN

Alexandria •   Jerusalem •

EGYPT   *SINAI*

6

LETTERS
TO THE
THESSALONIANS

1 THESSALONIANS (Acts 17:1-10)

When you are traveling, you will find that most hotels have a listing of the local Catholic Churches. You can go to one on a Sunday morning and find a community that shares your faith and commitment. It is a rare city in the world where such a community cannot be found. Before Christianity burst on the scene, the same was true of Judaism. A synagogue was to be found in almost every city of the known world.

Jesus sat down, called the Twelve and said to them, "If anyone wishes to be first, he shall be the last of all and the servant of all" (Mark 9:35).

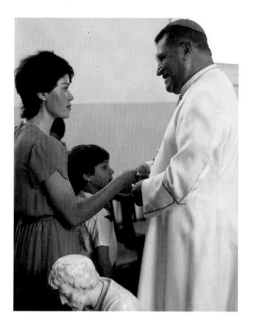

As was his custom in each city on his missionary journey, Paul made a bee line for the synagogue in Thessalonica. Naturally he found a congregation of Jews there. He preached to them. Distinguished visitors were usually asked to read a scripture passage and say a few words. He informed them that their search was ended, their hopes fulfilled. "He explained many things, showing that the Messiah had to suffer and rise from the dead: 'This Jesus I am telling you about is the Messiah '" (Acts 17:3). He convinced some of the faithful Jews, but also others who are identified in various translations as worshipping, sympathetic or God-fearing Greeks.

God-fearing People

The first Gentile convert made by Peter at Caesarea, the Roman Centurion Cornelius, is given the same title (Acts 10:1 ff). Apparently it was a whole class of people who attended the synagogue as admirers of Jewish monotheism and high ethical ideals.

However, because of the rigidity of the laws and the demand of circumcision, they would not go all the way to conversion. Paul's message of Jesus as the way to God without the Law or circumcision was music to their ears.

Some other Jews, however, were not happy with Paul's message, which was offensive to their orthodox beliefs. Failing to find Paul, they got a mob to drag some of his converts before the town meeting on the trumped-up charge of treason to the emperor and empire. A literal rendering of the Greek comes out: "These are the ones who are turning the world upside down" (Acts 17:6). If Paul had heard of it before he escaped from their clutches, he would have chuckled. His mission was just the reverse. He was living in an upside down world. With the Gospel he was turning it right side up.

Thank God for the opposition. Now Paul had to write and tell his hearers the rest of the message that had been so rudely cut short. They saved the letter for us. It is the earliest Christian writing, about fifteen years after the Resurrection. It gives us a good idea what life was like in that persecuted but vibrant Church.

Life Between the Times

The Thessalonian converts stood firm in their dynamic faith, effective love and unfailing hope in our Lord Jesus Christ. They took the Gospel seriously, not just as mere words, but as the very power of the Spirit at work in them, even though this stand brought on great trials. Evangelized by Paul, they promptly shared the Good News with their neighbors (1 Thessalonians 1:1 ff). On a return visit, Timothy, Paul's assistant, had checked things out and

sent back a report card with an A-
(chapter 3).

The minus was the result of two
misunderstandings. The first was about
the parousia or the second coming of
Jesus. The second concerned the
structure of the community.

First the structure (5:12-22): In the
history of Christianity there have
always been those who react to the
over-institutionalization or indeed the
over-clericalization of the Church. They
imply that we must return to the earliest
ideal of the Church which is a
charismatic, Spirit-centered, prophetic
community, unburdened with the
institutional structures and authority that
they find alien to it. This letter proves
that such an ideal is a caricature.

From the very beginning the
community was in need of structure and
authority. You might not like it, but
there would be chaos without it. Even
this early in the history of Christianity,
Paul had to warn his enthusiastic
converts: "We beg you, respect those
among you whose task it is to exercise
authority in the Lord and admonish you;
esteem them with the greatest love
because of their work" (5:12). But wise
as he was, Paul recognized that those in
charge can easily begin to think that
they are the only authentic channel of
God's will. There can emerge a
presumption that the Spirit speaks only
through them. Soon after urging respect
for the structure, he warns, "Do not
stifle the Spirit. Do not despise
prophecies" (5:19). Even the
evangelizer needs to be evangelized and
the voice for that can be, and frequently
is, other than the voice of the officers of
the Church. "The wind blows where it
will. You hear the sound it makes, but

*Paul was living in an
upside down world. With
the Gospel, he was
turning it right side up.*

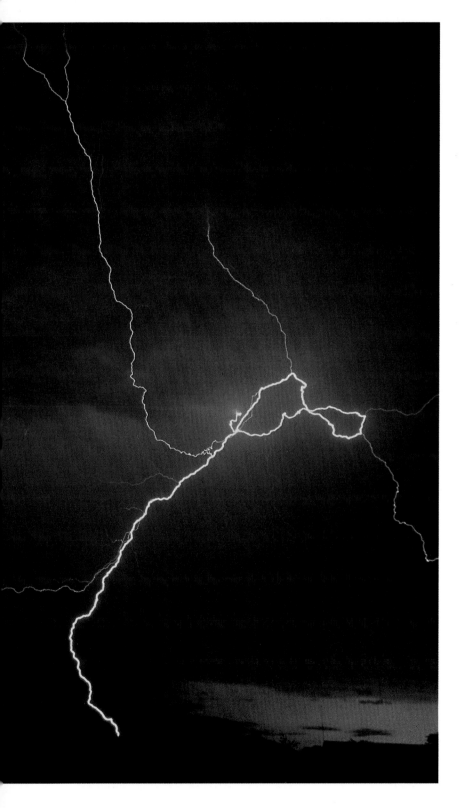

you do not know where it comes from or where it goes. So it is with everyone begotten of the Spirit" (John 3:8).

The other problem is one that the Church of Thessalonica shares with many fundamentalist Churches today. Flick the dial on the radio or the knob on television and you can hardly avoid hearing a proclamation that the end is at hand, Jesus is coming, Armageddon is near. It is amusing to hear those who claim to take the Bible literally ignore the assertion of Jesus that no one knows the day or the hour, not even himself (Mark 13:32). Today's preachers seem to know more than Jesus.

The problem in Paul's community (4:14-5:10) was that in their enthusiasm they thought that Jesus had misplaced his appointment calendar. He had been understood to say that the second coming would occur before that generation passed away. They had been to the wakes, and they knew that their generation was passing away. Where was Jesus? His delay gave rise to several questions.

Reshaping Society

Having misunderstood the timing, had they misunderstood the reality also? Would there even be a second coming? As surely as we affirm at Mass, Paul knew: "Christ has died, Christ is risen, Christ will come again." The second coming is an integral and important part of the gospel message. He cites their own experience: "You turned to God from idols, to serve him who is the living and true God and to await from heaven the Son he raised from the dead" (1 Thessalonians 1:9).

Then what was it going to be like? Once again Paul taps into their

"Then I saw a new heaven and a new earth....I heard a loud voice from the throne saying, 'Behold, God's dwelling is with the human race'" *(Revelation 21:1,3).*

(photo left) "I think that the purpose and cause of the Incarnation was that the Lord might illuminate the world by divine wisdom and excite it to the love of God" (Peter Abelard).

experience. They knew that when there was trouble or dissension in one of the imperial colonies, the emperor would send a representative to restore order and maintain peace. His coming (Greek = parousia) was heralded by a trumpet blast, and the loyal citizens would be caught up in enthusiasm (raptured) and hasten forth to welcome him. For Paul this scenario was an analogy of what the parousia would be like. It was not a literal description of it. The point is that Jesus the Lord will come to establish his Reign of justice and peace for his faithful followers. The point is not that they will be tiptoeing around on the clouds. That is the arrogant misinterpretation of those who drive around with a bumper sticker proclaiming: "In the event of the rapture this car will be unoccupied."

Finally, granted that the parousia might not be right around the corner, how should we live "as we wait in joyful hope for the coming of our Savior, Jesus Christ"?

Sleepers sleep by night and drunkards drink by night. We who live by day must be alert putting on faith and love as a breastplate and the hope of salvation as a helmet. God has not destined us for wrath but for acquiring salvation through our Lord Jesus Christ (1 Thessalonians 5:7-9).

The early Church, as the Church must ever be, was aware, alert, expectant, on tiptoe. While working to transform this upside down world into God's Reign, we wait with bated breath for Jesus to complete the work he began. Paul's communities yearned for that with such passion that they didn't even pause to translate their prayer from the Aramaic, "Maranatha!" (1 Cor 16:22). As part of the Gospel, it must always be the prayer of the pilgrim Church journeying to our completion in the Reign of God: "O Lord, come!"

2 THESSALONIANS

The Word of God is usually a solution to a problem. This letter is an exception. It is a problem. Read it backwards and the problem is evident. The last lines are: "This greeting is in my own hand, Paul's. This is the sign in every

(photo right)   "...truth stumbles in the public square..." (Isaiah 59:14).

(photo right)   "...truth stumbles in the public square..." (Isaiah 59:14).

letter"(3:17). Me thinks he doth protest too much. You and I, when writing a letter, simply sign it. Paul usually does the same. At the end of Romans, he mentions that the actual writing is being done by a secretary, but the protestation of authenticity at the end of 2 Thessalonians is suspicious.

The plot thickens when we realize that chapters 1 and 3, for the most part, seem to have been copied from 1 Thessalonians. Chapter 2 is not only quite different from 1 Thessalonians, it is very different from what Paul says in all of his other writings. It does contain a favorite theme of Paul, the parousia, but with some very strange elements that seem alien to his thought.

The letter seems to have been written by someone using Paul's name, to lend authority to his words, in order to solve a problem: overzealous hope in the coming of Jesus has grown into infallible certainty that it is right around the corner.

> We ask you, with regard to the coming (parousia) of our Lord Jesus Christ, and our assembling with him (rapture), not to be shaken out of your minds suddenly, or to be alarmed either by a Spirit, or by an oral statement, or by a letter allegedly from us to the effect that the day of the Lord is at hand (2 Thessalonians 2:1-2).

We don't need Sherlock Holmes to uncover that clue. Someone has been trying to speak in Paul's name.

Messenger or Deceiver?

The writer of this letter is, in effect, saying to the alarmist who is confusing the Thessalonians, "Whatever you can do, I can do better." It is difficult to decide whether he is part of the solution or part of the problem. His reason for the delay of the parousia is not usually what we hear from Paul:

> Let no one deceive you in any way. For unless the apostasy comes first and the lawless one is revealed, the one doomed to perdition, who opposes and exalts himself above every so-called god and object of worship, so as to seat himself in the temple of God, claiming that he is a god - do you not recall that while I was still with you, I told you these things? And now you know what is restraining, that he may be revealed in his time. For the mystery of lawlessness is already at work. But the one who restrains is to do so only for the present, until he is removed from the scene. And then the lawless one will be revealed, whom the Lord (Jesus) will kill with the breath of his mouth and render powerless by the manifestation of his coming (parousia), the one whose coming springs from the power of Satan in every mighty deed and in signs and wonders that lie, and in every wicked deceit for those who are perishing because they have not accepted the love of truth so that they may be saved. Therefore, God is sending them a deceiving power so that they may believe the lie (2 Thessalonians 2:3-13).

"Christ has turned all our sunsets into dawns" (Clement of Alexandria).

Wow! How unlike Paul that sounds. Nowhere else does he speak of the "lawless one." As a matter of fact Paul himself is suspected of being "lawless" by fellow Christians because he sees that Jesus replaces the Law.

He says that we know what is restraining the lawless one. We don't, and we haven't the slightest clue. The whole passage is easily understood as a frightful determinism in which free will has no place, since even God sends a deceiving power. What chance have we mere mortals if almighty God does that?

No, our loving God does not deceive, nor does he allow a deceiver to overpower any of us. It seems what we have here is someone trying to calm down an overly enthusiastic community. Whether or not he succeeded and the community perceived a meaning in his words that is hidden from us, we have no way of knowing. The message that this inspired Word does convey to us is that sometimes God's Word was intended uniquely to address a community situation of old

and may have been meant only for that time. Such was the case with the inspired laws of the Old Testament which are no longer in effect.

If there is one lesson that we can learn from it, it may well be that we should take with a grain of salt the TV evangelists of today who grab on to these texts as if they were written only for our own times without reference to yesterday.

No matter how confusing the language, the fact remains certain that Jesus is Lord. He's in charge, and even while he was on earth he broke the power of Satan and told his disciples that he saw him falling from heaven. The last line of this epistle says it all: "The grace of our Lord Jesus Christ be with all of you."

7

LETTERS TO THE PHILIPPIANS AND THE GALATIANS

PHILIPPIANS

Philip, the father of Alexander the Great, would have been amazed that his enduring fame rests not so much on his accomplishments, nor on a city named after him, but on a letter written to the Christian community of that city.

It is not even a letter actually; it's a thank-you note. Paul was in jail in Ephesus. Try to picture the grateful smile on his face when a care package arrives from those he has brought to the faith in Philippi. What can he send them back to thank them? They have helped to make his time in jail more tolerable. He will help to make their life in Christ more understandable.

To do this, he develops three words; *community, Lord, freedom*. But there is a fourth word that brings them all together: *joy*. Reading through the letter, notice how often the word joy or rejoicing is used. And this is from a man in prison because of his witness to Christ! "Indeed, I shall continue to rejoice for I know that this will result in deliverance for me through your prayers and support from the Spirit of Jesus Christ" (1:19).

Partnership

Being in jail, he has leisure time to meditate on the Christian vocation. First he shares with them the meaning of the word, *community*. The Greek is *koinonia* and is sometimes translated as partnership or fellowship (1:3). The word implies such an intimacy that in the Old Testament it was never used of God and his people. The distant God could not be spoken of as having koinonia, community, with his far away people. Paul's own experience in Christ on the road to Damascus made him

aware of how close this God had come to us in Jesus. Koinonia becomes one of his favorite words to express the reality of our intimacy, closeness, oneness in Jesus. He tries to find every synonym he can to spell out the reality. Koinonia is community. It's fellowship. It's Church. It's the Body of Christ.

This reality is achieved in the second word he develops. It is *Lord:* Jesus Christ, the Word made flesh.

Remember that Paul never knew Jesus before the Lord's resurrection. He only knew him by the same faith that we know him. What struck him was the reality that the Son of God with all his divine dignity and glory did not think that it was something to be clung to, grasped at, or to be miserly about. He let go and became one of us. A missionary from Japan once mentioned that there are few converts among the Japanese. But when they do convert, they are totally amazed, excited and enthused that God sent his Son as one of us. We, who have taken it for granted that the "Word was made flesh," could well learn from the Japanese. Paul reminds us of that. "He emptied himself, taking the form of a slave, coming in human likeness, and found in human appearance" (2:6). Notice in your Bible, that this section is set off as poetry. Whether this was a hymn that the Philippians were familiar with and were already singing or that Paul wrote for this letter, we are not sure. We can be sure, however, that its content is worth singing about: The self-emptying of the Son of God to take on the lowest form of our humanity, slavery and death as a criminal, is not the end. The Father has the last word and it is exaltation. That is why every Christian with a voice must accept, acknowledge and sing the new title: "Jesus Christ is Lord."

Freedom

In chapter 3, Paul begins to develop the theme that preoccupied him and the infant Church for decades. It is summed up in one word: *freedom.* Freedom from the Law. Freedom to let the Lord and not the Law control our lives. Freedom to grow in a community of faith and love and not in a group that marched in lock-step to the martial commands of the Law.

For Paul, if the Law is in charge, then Jesus is not! He is not Lord! If the Law unites us, then we are not one as the Body of Christ. Without freedom from the Law, there is no Church, there is no lordship of Jesus.

Paul is not talking theoretical theology or abstract speculation. He has been down the road, and it is not his opinion but his very experience that he shares. While guideline and ritual may be important and even necessary to religion, they are not the essence of it. The heart of religion is personal

relationship with God. The demands of that may be spelled out in Law and the joy of it may be celebrated in ritual, but neither one can substitute for the love and faith with which God binds us to himself. Paul knows. He had been a Pharisee and he's not going to make the same mistake again. He wrote this thank you note to keep the Philippians and ourselves from falling into the same trap out of which the outstretched hand of Jesus had lifted him.

GALATIANS

It would have been an extraordinary experience to have been a fly on the wall when the Galatian Christians, gathered for the Breaking of the Bread, heard this letter read for the first time. Paul is really angry with them; but even more, he is livid with rage at the Judaizers. They are the Jewish Christians from Jerusalem, dogging his footsteps, checking on his orthodoxy and insinuating to his converts that he is a false apostle who preaches a watered down Gospel.

In all his other letters, Paul starts out with praise and thanksgiving for the faith of the community. No time for that here. Paul gets right down to business: the defense of his mission as an apostle, and the truth of his Gospel. He has been sent by Jesus Christ and God his Father. He is a card carrying apostle and he has the same call and credentials as the rest of them (1:1).

In response to the accusation that he is preaching cheap grace, making it easy to be Christian by doing away with the demands of the Law, he insists that the message he preaches is not of his making. "I assure you, the Gospel I proclaimed to you is no mere human invention. I did not get it from any

*"Mission is the church
in love with the whole
world" (Charles L.
Slattery).*

*(photo: facing page)
"You must know that
your body is a temple of
the Holy Spirit who is
within....So glorify God
in your body" (1
Corinthians 6:19 ff).*

person nor was I schooled in it. It came
by revelation from Jesus Christ" (1:11).

On the contrary, he insists that it is his
accusers who are preaching "another"
and, therefore, "false" Gospel. For Paul
the Gospel is Jesus. Period. For the
Judaizers, the Gospel is Jesus and the
Law. Paul is so upset about this
distortion that he tells the Galatians that
even if the angel who first gave the Law
to Moses shows up again, they are to
pay no attention to him.

As for those preaching "another
Gospel," most translations have Paul
saying let them be accursed or
anathema. What he is really saying is
that he wishes they would go to hell,
because that is where they are trying to
lead the Galatians (1:6-9).

Two-Track Christianity?

Paul will not mince his words because
he is convinced that nothing less than
Gospel, grace, the Reign of God and
indeed the Lordship of Jesus Christ are
at stake. The bottom line of chapter 2 is
also the bottom line of Paul's position:

> The life I live now is not my own;
> Christ is living in me. I still live my
> human life, but it is a life of faith in
> the Son of God, who loved me, and
> gave himself for me. I will not treat
> God's gracious gift as pointless. If
> justice is available through the law,
> then Christ died to no purpose
> (Galatians 2:20-21).

So certain is he of his position that
Paul doesn't hesitate to accuse Peter of
misleading people. Peter had been
eating bacon with the Gentile
Christians, but quickly went kosher
when the Jewish Christians appeared.
He gave the impression that there was a
two track Christianity which had a strict
form with rules and regulations for one
group (obviously the superior one!) and
freedom from the Law for the other.
Two gospels, two spiritualities, two
kinds of discipleship, two different
ways to God. It was all one too many
for Paul.

In chapter 3, he turns on the Galatians
who have fallen for this nonsense. They
had heard him preach. They should
know better:

> Stupid Galatians. Who has bewitched
> you?... I want to learn only this from
> you: Did you receive the Spirit from
> works of the law or from faith in
> what you heard? Are you so stupid?
> After beginning with the Spirit are
> you now ending with the flesh? (3:1-
> 3).

The Spirit is God's power and the
flesh is mere weak, human activity. If
that is all we have to work with, then
we'd better quickly cry: "God help us."
In chapters 3 and 4, Paul marshals
every argument imaginable to show that
the Law, once given by God, was given
for a time, but now, in the fullness of
time, it is no longer necessary, operable
or in force. Indeed, as the Judaizers
have shown, it can be dangerous and
destructive of the Gospel.

Life Without Commandments?

Paul now has a major problem. In rejecting legalism - the Law as a means for salvation, he has also thrown out the only guide for morality that the people had. If the commandments are gone, does that mean that I can do as I please? Such an accusation has been made against Paul, that he is a moral anarchist. The problem of those who make the accusation is that they have confused morality with the Law and commandments.

Law is the spelling out of the demands of a relationship. There are certain things that will help, and certain things that will harm a relationship. Mature people know what they are. Immature people need someone to spell them out in laws. That is why Paul's analogies about the Law refer to immaturity. We needed it as a guardian until we were old enough to run our own affairs by ourselves (4:1). It was also our baby sitter (monitor) until we were mature enough to be trusted to take care of ourselves (3:25).

That's a nice argument, but what is to be our guide if the Law and commandments are no longer in effect? Paul sees three alternatives. You can go back, you can go in, or you can go out.

You can go back, you can become a slave of the Law again. You can act like a child who always needs someone to tell you what to do. You can identify morality with external behavior, which is all the Law can regulate. This whole emphasis on legalism is associated with circumcision. Paul rather indelicately gives his opinion of this whole approach when he says: "Would that those who are troubling you might go the whole way and castrate themselves"

There is an old philosophical principle that puts it very succinctly: Beings act according to their nature.

(5:12). If circumcision is virtue, why not go all the way to heroic virtue?

Paul will not go back. Neither will he go in. What is within is just me. Most translations call it the "flesh" (5:13-21). It is me, in all my selfishness, self-centeredness, human weakness and meager resources that cries out: "I gotta be me. I gotta do my own thing." And my own thing is me, with no regard for anyone else. The result? "If you go on biting and tearing each other to pieces, take care. You will end up in mutual destruction" (5:15). Replacing slavery to the Law with slavery to selfishness is a move from the frying pan into the fire. Paul tells us what happens when your guiding principle is just you (the flesh):

> It is obvious what proceeds from the flesh: lewd conduct, impurity, licentiousness, idolatry, sorcery, hostilities, bickering, outbursts of rage, selfish rivalries, dissensions, factions, envy, drunkenness, orgies, and the like (Galatians 5:19).

There is an old philosophical principle that puts it very succinctly: Beings act according to their nature. If we are merely human flesh, our activity will reflect that. Don't expect more than selfish, divisive, alienating, grabbing, self-aggrandizing activity.

The Alternative

There is the third alternative. We can reject both Law and flesh and go out to the Spirit. We can open up and let the Holy Spirit of Jesus Christ take over our lives. The Spirit is the new guide that takes over our lives and activities. We no longer ask of an action, is it lawful? We ask how this will help me to grow in Christ and bring greater love to the community. "Out of love, place yourselves at one another's service. The whole Law has found its fulfillment in this one saying: 'You shall love your neighbor as yourself'" (5:13). "Since we live by the Spirit, let us follow the Spirit's lead" (5:25).

Paul's detractors said he watered down the Gospel's demands by throwing out the Law. On the contrary. Paul's Gospel is much more demanding. As a matter of fact, it demands that we grow up and ask the right questions. The question is no longer,"What does the Law require of us?" The question is, "What does Jesus require of us?" That may seem tough and even nebulous, but Jesus promised he would not leave us orphans. He said he would send the Spirit. Jesus never reneged on a promise. Paul knew that. So will we if we will go out to the Spirit and allow him to take over. We can go back (to the Law) go in (to the flesh) or out (to the Spirit).

This letter of Paul has been called the Magna Carta of Christian freedom. It is certainly that. Paul initiated the struggle to return religion to love and to keep Law in its place. Exalting Law over the love of Christ will always be one of

"Out of love, place yourselves at one another's service" (Galatians 5:13).

those idols that Pope Paul VI spoke of in his marvelous encyclical on evangelization: "The Church is the People of God immersed in the world, and often tempted by idols. This means that she has a constant need of being evangelized, if she wishes to retain freshness, vigor and strength in order to proclaim the Gospel."

LETTERS TO THE CORINTHIANS

1 CORINTHIANS

P oor Paul. The Church at the headquarters in Jerusalem suspects him. The people to whom he has brought the Gospel misunderstand him. One would think that he would have sought out a calm, peaceful country parish where the only problem was raising the Sunday collection. Not Paul. He's driven by the Gospel. It takes him to Corinth, which was known as the "Sin City" of the ancient world. It was one big combat zone and red light district.

The immorality of the port city of Corinth was proverbial in the Roman empire. Everyone just took it for granted that Corinthians had the morals of an alley cat.

The situation was compounded by the fact that Corinth was the center of a philosophical and religious revival. The philosophers, however, were more interested in the bodies of their students than their minds. And the religious revival was twofold. The temple of the goddess Aphrodite employed five hundred cultic prostitutes to satisfy the "religious needs" of the community.

Also, every sailor that arrived back in this cross-roads of the Roman empire brought news of all the new oriental religions that promised salvation, fulfillment and satisfaction. But these were not for everyone, only for the chosen few, as opposed to the run of the mill crowd.

It is a wonder that Paul was even listened to at all. The fact of the matter is that he was only half listened to. Some Corinthians heard what they wanted to hear and forgot or ignored the rest. This created many problems, and that's why this letter was written.

Ten Problems

PROBLEM ONE: The Body of Christ divided. The first chapter reveals that the Corinthians were like some modern day television Christians who switch channels until they find their favorite evangelist. Then they stay glued to the tube, becoming disciples of one particular evangelist, saying "Amen" to his or her every utterance and appeal. The Corinthians had their own favorites, some pledging allegiance to Cephas (Peter), others to Apollos, others to Paul and, strangely enough, some to Christ. Paul put an end to this popularity contest. "Has Christ then been divided into parts? Was it Paul who was crucified for you? Was it in Paul's name that you were baptized?" (1:13). We are disciples of the message, not the messenger. Jesus is the message. He is the Gospel.

PROBLEM TWO: Mystery religions. At the same time that Christianity was sweeping the world, another new kind of religion, imported from the mysterious orient, was gaining in popularity. This was the "mystery" religion that promised secret access to salvation and the revelation of hidden "knowledge" to the few chosen initiates. It was a snob religion, for the few. Since there's a bit of snob in everyone of us, it had a strong appeal for those who already considered themselves above the common horde. The problem arose when some Corinthians wanted to use this approach as a model for Christianity.

They wanted a gospel that contained revelation of "mysteries" and the unveiling of special "knowledge" or "wisdom" for the initiated few, and another gospel for the run of the mill crowd. Everyone likes to have the inside track, whether it be in the stock market, a special sale, or religion.

Paul rejects this snobbery by insisting (chapters 1-4) that there is a mystery. It is Jesus. There is special knowledge. It is of Jesus. There is wisdom. It is found in Jesus. "We preach Christ crucified - a stumbling block to the Jews and an absurdity to the Gentiles; but to those who are called, Jews and Greeks alike, Christ, the power of God and the wisdom of God" (1:24).

PROBLEM THREE: Doing what comes naturally. As in all of the Churches, Paul preached freedom in Corinth. Freedom from the Law. Freedom to come to Jesus. Some of the community were spiritually impaired of hearing and only heard the first part. For them the Good News was that there were no restraints. They interpreted Paul's message to be that Christianity was a religion of creed and cult, but no code. Several of the community lost no time in putting this ethics-free religion into practice.

One man began sleeping with his stepmother in the name of gospel freedom. The situation was so bad that the rest of the community thought that his conduct was compatible with the Gospel. "Religion is such a private thing, you know."

Another man, blissfully unaware that there are Christian standards of behavior based on love, brought a lawsuit against a fellow Christian in a pagan court. Pagan principles of morality and ethics were good enough for him.

The third one really hit bottom. He came out with a couple of slogans.

"Everything is lawful for me." Paul's reply? "Everything is lawful for me, but that does not mean that everything is good for me, nor will I let myself be enslaved by anything" (6:12). That didn't stop our enterprising Corinthian. He came out with another slogan: "Food is for the stomach and the stomach is for food." No problem there. Who would have any difficulty about the functions of the natural organs of the body? Having achieved consensus on that point, the innovator said that there was another organ that should be kept well exercised and there was nothing wrong with fornication. Obviously all of the Corinthians' problems were not intellectual. Some were below the belt! More obviously, Paul, who began the whole fiasco by his preaching of Christian freedom, has a major problem. Should he back off in the light of these abuses that he says

"Throughout history even to the present day, there is found among different peoples a certain awareness of a hidden power, which lies behind the course of nature and the events of human life" (Vatican Council II, 1965).

wouldn't even be found among the pagans? Should he tell them that the time of renewal and experimentation is over and they should go back to the good old days of law and order? Should he tell them that he has found serious deficiencies in their catechetical training? Should he insist that they wouldn't be acting the way they are if they knew their commandments?

None of the above. For Paul, morality does not depend on law. It depends on love and a relationship with Jesus Christ. He tells them that they wouldn't be behaving the way they are if they knew who they were. "The body is not for immorality but for the Lord... Do you not know that your bodies are members of Christ? Shall I take Christ's members and make them the members of a prostitute? Of course not!... Do you not know that your own body is a temple of the Holy Spirit who is within you, whom you have from

God. You are not your own. You have been purchased, and at a price. So glorify God in your Body" (6:13 ff).

For Paul, gospel freedom is not moral anarchy. It is freedom to come to Jesus and let him be Lord of our actions.

PROBLEM FOUR: Sex and the Christian (chapter 7). A terrible misunderstanding of Paul's teaching can arise if the first lines of chapter 7 are attributed to him. They are not his thought at all. They are a statement of a problem in Corinth that the community wrote to him about. Some members of the Church were saying: "A man is better off having no relations with a woman. But to avoid immorality, every man should have his own wife and every woman her own husband." Those Corinthians! One of them just implied that the best way to get rid of temptation is to give in to it. Now another one says that even in marriage, sex is barely

tolerable. Unbridled license and negative, ascetical abstinence - both in the name of the Gospel.

Paul does think that in the light of the impending and imminent (so he thinks) parousia, celibacy is to be preferred. If the end of the world is around the corner, it is better to prepare for it than to spend the time hiring a reception hall and sending out invitations. But Paul is not stubbornly insistent. To be so would interfere with God's call and gift. Concerning celibacy and marriage, he writes: "Each one has a particular gift from God, one of one kind and one of another" (7:7). Marriage is a gift (the Greek word is charism) every bit as holy, necessary and helpful to the community as celibacy. Sex in marriage is integral to that gift and not just something to be tolerated as a deterrent to immorality.

PROBLEM FIVE: "I've got my rights" (chapters 8, 9, 10). This may seem like a silly problem. It comes down to this. In a city where every animal is sacrificed in the pagan temple before being put on the butcher block, is vegetarianism the only option for Christians? No problem, says Paul. An idol is nothing and meat that has been offered to nothing is perfectly O.K. for Christians. Enjoy your hamburger. You have a right to eat that meat. Simple enough.

But the plot thickens. Enter a recent convert, weak in faith, who is not yet certain that there is one God and that idols are nothing. He sees you exercising your right to eat meat. He concludes that one can be a Christian and still live like the pagans, even participating in their ritual. You know there is nothing to the idol, and you are only exercising your right. But, writes

Marriage is a gift (the Greek word is charism) every bit as holy, necessary and helpful to the community as celibacy.

Paul, "because of your `knowledge' the weak one perishes, that brother or sister for whom Christ died. When you sin thus against your brothers or sisters and wound their weak consciences, you are sinning against Christ" (8:11). For a Christian, morality is not just avoiding what is immoral. It may mean giving up a legitimate right to avoid the appearance of immorality. It means having a delicate sensitivity to where the other members of the community are and helping them to grow to maturity.

Question: "Why should my liberty be restricted by another's conscience?"

Answer: The fact is that whether you eat or drink - whatever you do - you should do all for the glory of God. Give no offense to Jew or Greek or to the Church of God, just as I try to please all, in any way I can, by seeking not my own advantage but that of the many, that they may be saved. Imitate me as I imitate Christ (10:31 ff).

PROBLEM SIX: Of long hair and veils (11:1-16). This is one place where Paul is rather clear and straightforward on the solution. We are just not sure

*(Photo: facing page)
"Tell me how much you
know of the sufferings of
your fellow human beings
and I will tell you how
much you have loved
them" (Helmut
Thielicke).*

what the problem was. Why was it so important that women should have their heads covered when they led the prayers or preached to the community? Was it because the street walkers of Corinth walked around with tresses blowing in the breeze and Paul didn't want the women of his community to get a reputation by association? We don't know, but it should not be missed that he acknowledges their right to lead the prayer and to preach to the community. He puts into practice his statement of Galatians 3:28: "There does not exist among you Jew or Greek, slave or freeman, male or female. All are one in Christ Jesus."

It did not take the Church long to draw back from Paul's liberal position on the role of women. He was only following in the footsteps of his Lord who did the unheard of thing of admitting them to discipleship. But even the generation after Paul was not comfortable with that. In 14:33 someone, still hung up on the Law (and Paul was not), snuck in a couple of sentences, contradicting his affirmation in chapter 11, yet trying to get his name and authority behind his own chauvinistic prejudice. He (not Paul) wrote:

> According to the rule observed in all the assemblies of the believers, women should keep silent in such gatherings. They may not speak. Rather, as the law states, submissiveness is indicated for them. If they want to learn anything, they should ask their husbands at home. It is a disgrace when a woman speaks in the assembly (1 Corinthians 14:33-5).

That's the prohibition of the synagogue, not the freedom Paul found in the Church.

PROBLEM SEVEN: When going to church is a sin (11:17-34). The Mass has not yet had its silver anniversary and it has become a problem in Corinth. Like the Last Supper, it was celebrated in the context of a meal. It was a covered dish dinner with each one making a contribution and concluding with the Breaking of the Bread, the Eucharist.

The poor, who couldn't afford the food, waited outside until the end. The big hearted Corinthians were willing to share a bit of bread and wine. Sharing the meal was a bit too much to ask. Paul is the master of understatement when he says: "Your meetings are not profitable but harmful." As a matter of fact they were disastrous and sinful. The sacrament of unity and communion was used to promote disunity and alienation. It was a counter sign.

Paul tells them that their problem is that they fail to recognize the Body. They probably thought at first that he was accusing them of not affirming the Body of Christ on the altar. Their faith wasn't that weak! But Paul uses the word, Body, with intentional ambiguity. In 10:17 he had told them: "We, many though we are, are one Body, for we all partake of the one loaf." In the very next chapter he insists: "You then are the Body of Christ. Everyone of you is a member of it" (12:27). Their problem was not so much with the Body of Christ on the altar as with the Body of Christ around the altar. They are like people today who see the light of the tabernacle lamp and say, "Jesus is here." But they are unable to see the light in their neighbor's eye and say, "Jesus is here."

PROBLEM EIGHT: The whole Church is charismatic (chapters 12, 13, 14). At the very beginning of this letter Paul had already acknowledged the

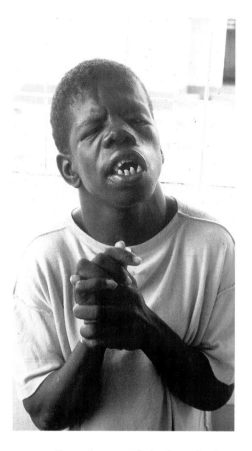

12:11 They can't be earned or claimed, for they are gifts of the Spirit who distributes them at will.

12:25 It is a sign of their abuse when the gifts cause dissension in the community, leading to a lack of concern for one another.

12:31 There is a hierarchy in their value. "Set your heart on the greater gifts." In Paul's listing, wisdom, preaching and faith rate high (12:8). Tongues and their interpretation come last (12:12).

14:48 There may be a dependence of one gift upon another. For example, if there is no one to interpret, there should be no speaking in tongues.

14:32 The gifts are under the control of the recipient, "since God is not a God of disorder but of peace."

13:1-13 They are all worse than useless and may even be destructive if they are not permeated with, operative through, and vivified by, the greatest charism of all: love.

PROBLEM NINE: The resurrection (chapter 15). Amazingly enough the problem of the resurrection in chapter 15 is closely allied to the problems of morality, sex, and marriage in chapters 3 and 4. They all have the same starting point which is the neo-platonic philosophical point of view then current in Corinth. It held that the soul was the prisoner of the body and that we would never be truly free until we escaped the shackles of the body. It was an obstacle and impediment to growth, spirituality and union with God. If the body is such a negative influence, then we can suppress its demands by giving in to them or by stifling them with asceticism. That was the problem Paul confronted on morality, sex and marriage.

extraordinary legacy of charisms in the Corinthian community. "I continually thank my God for you because of the favor he has bestowed on you in Christ Jesus, in whom you have been richly endowed with every gift of speech and knowledge" (1:4). Later on he affirms that charisms are not the private preserve of a few: "Each one has a particular gift from God" (7:7). Every Christian is gifted, is charismatic.

In these chapters Paul insists on certain characteristics of these gifts and on guidelines for their use:

12:2 They are not irrational, merely emotional impulses.

12:4 There is a great variety of them.

12:7 They are a manifestation of the Holy Spirit, not intended for the individual but for the ministry of building up the Church.

Now, the supposed evil and detrimental role of the body takes a different twist. If the body is so bad, who wants it resurrected? Of course, this premise is false. The body is not bad. The proclamation that the Word was made flesh and dwelt among us puts an end to that nonsense.

The Corinthians have taken their own philosophy to its ultimate conclusion. They are wrong. Now Paul takes the Gospel to its ultimate conclusion with every argument he can muster. If there is no resurrection for us, then there was none for Jesus. And then we are worse off than the pagans, for we are still in our sins. All we have is some insightful teachings of a perceptive prophet from Galilee. No, since Jesus is risen, we are risen, renewed and changed. There is a promise for the future, as well as hope in the present. We don't just have a collection of teachings, we have the risen Lord Jesus and he won't let us down.

PROBLEM TEN: Helping another community (chapter 16). Paul's letter concludes with the collection for the Church in Jerusalem, which was suffering a great famine. The generous support offered by Gentile Christians to Jewish Christians served as a concrete sign of their new-found fellowship.

2 CORINTHIANS

If you have ever had difficulties with the postal service you can sympathize with the mix-up in Paul's Corinthian correspondence. In 1 Corinthians 5:9, he mentions a previous letter that he wrote to them. We're not sure they received it. If they did, the mail service out of Corinth must have been rather poor. We haven't received it.

Then some "envelopes" must have gotten lost. The one containing 2 Corinthians has three letters and one of them wasn't even written by Paul. 2 Corinthians 10-13 is a separate letter sent after a second visit by Paul to Corinth. It is called the angry letter. 2 Corinthians 1-9 was sent by Paul a little later after an unsuccessful attempt to make a third visit to his Church there. 2 Corinthians 6:14-7:1 is a note from someone else that got sandwiched in the midst of Paul's inverted letters. It is so contrary to Paul's tone, thought and practice that it could not have been written by him. This may seem a bit confused (It is!) and confusing (It need not be!). If the chapters are read in this order, they will make a lot more sense.

Paul Responds

The angry letter (2 Corinthians 10-13) resulted from Paul's disappointment after a second pastoral visit to Corinth. Apparently he went to check up on the community to determine if the problems exposed in his previous letter, I Corinthians, had been resolved. The troublemakers responsible for the tension, disunity and polarization in the community were just waiting for him. It must have been a very unpleasant scene. Paul was accused of being two-faced. "His letters, they say, are severe and forceful, but when he is here in person he is unimpressive and his word makes no great impact" (10:1). He accuses them of lack of fidelity. "When someone comes preaching another Jesus than the one we preached...or a gospel other than the Gospel you accepted, you seem to endure it quite well" (11:4). They questioned his authority, trying to drive a wedge between him and other members of the Church (11:5). "I

"No society can live at peace with itself, or with the world, without a full awareness of the worth and dignity of every human person, and of the sacredness of all human life" (United States Bishops' Pastoral Letter on Peace).

consider myself inferior to the superior apostles in nothing." He threw in their faces the fact that he hadn't even been financially supported by them (11:7). He is forced to present his credentials detailing all the suffering the preaching of the Gospel has brought him. Of course, the implication is that the physical suffering was a tea party compared to what they are now doing to him.

Yet even in this physical, psychological and emotional abuse the power of the Lord is at work (12:10). "I am content with weakness, with mistreatment, with distress, with persecutions and difficulties for the sake of Christ; for when I am powerless, it is then that I am strong" (12:10). Exasperated with them and himself for meeting anger with anger, he cries out:

What a fool I have become! You have driven me to it (2 Corinthians 12:11).

Do you think throughout this recital that I am defending myself to you? Before God I tell you, in Christ, I have done everything to build you up, my dear ones. I fear that when I come I may not find you to my liking, nor may you find me to yours (12:19). He challenges them: Test yourselves to see whether you are living in faith; examine yourselves. Perhaps you yourselves do not realize that Christ Jesus is in you - unless of course, you have failed the challenge (13:5).

With all that is going on in the community (discord, jealousy, outbursts of rage, selfish ambitions, slander and gossip, self importance and disorder [12:20]), the bottom line is a questioning of Paul's authority. He is ready for detractors: "I am writing in this way while away from you, so that when I am with you I may not have to exercise with severity the authority the Lord has given me - authority to build up, rather than tear down" (13:10).

He never did get back to Corinth, but his later letter indicates that his last wish in this one was fulfilled: "Mend your ways. Encourage one another. Live in harmony and peace, and the God of love and peace will be with you" (13:11).

Letter of Reconciliation

That later letter which is now found in 2 Corinthians 1-9 has a much different tone. In it he even almost, but not quite, apologizes for the tone of the previous letter. "I wrote you in great sorrow and anguish, with copious tears - not to make you sad, but to help you realize the great love I bear you" (2:4). If he doesn't quite have his tail between his legs, at least he has calmed down and is ready to share with them his deepening understanding of the Gospel:

> It is not ourselves that we preach, but Christ Jesus as Lord, and ourselves as your servants for Jesus' sake. For God, who said, `Let light shine out of darkness,' has shone in our hearts, that we in turn might make known the glory of God shining on the face of Christ. This treasure we possess in earthen vessels to make it clear that its surpassing power comes from God and not from us (2 Corinthinas 4:5).

If Paul was a scrapper, he was not one to walk around with a chip on his shoulder. Nor did he hold a grudge, even though his personal integrity and ministry had been vilified. No matter what happened it could not stop him from preaching the Gospel.

It would be nice to say, "All's well that ends well," but the story isn't over. When the collection of the Corinthian letters was put together, someone inserted a passage in chapter 6. It is an obvious interruption in the text and line of thought. With it removed, the passage reads smoothly: 6:14 "Open wide your hearts." Then skip to 7:2 "Make room for us in your hearts." Paul's train of thought has been interrupted by 6:14 to 7:1. This passage is contrary to Paul's own practice. It tells them to avoid unbelievers. If that were his advice and he had followed it, he never would have made a convert. He's the Apostle to the Gentiles.

Also, there are several words in here that are not part of Paul's vocabulary in all the rest of his writings. Most noticeable is "Belial." He frequently speaks of Satan, but never uses Belial. The phrase "separate yourselves and touch nothing unclean (not kosher)" is strange advice indeed supposedly on the lips of one who has thrown out the Law!

This passage, neither Pauline nor Christian, may have been inserted by the same hand that put in his own two cents in 1 Corinthians 14, forbidding women to speak in church. Footnotes in some modern Bibles indicate that it was a convert from the Essenes at Qumran. It corresponds exactly to their teaching, but not to Paul's.

9

LETTER TO
THE ROMANS

Most people don't write personal
letters to people they have never
met. But that is what Paul does when he
writes to the Romans. He has never been to
Rome, doesn't know what the problems of the
community are, and has no authority over the
Roman Church. Apparently he feels
constrained to write the letter because he is
nervous that rumors and half-truths about
himself and his preaching have preceded him.
He is on his way there and wants to set the
record straight. His experience in

"Love one another with mutual affection ....Rejoice with those who rejoice, weep with those who weep" (Romans 12:10,15).

Galatia and Corinth have made him gun-shy, and he wants to clear the air so he won't have to spend all his time defending himself when he arrives.

He writes ahead with a complete and detailed treatment of his beliefs. He tells them:

> God is my witness, whom I serve with my spirit in proclaiming the Gospel of his Son, that I remember you constantly, always asking in my prayers that somehow by God's will I may at last find my way clear to come to you. For I long to see you, that I may share with you some spiritual gift so that you and I may be mutually encouraged by one another's faith, yours and mine (1:9-12).

Notice the emphasis on common faith. He wants to assure them that his faith is the same as theirs, all rumors to the contrary.

In this letter he shares that faith, faith in Jesus Christ. But the question is, why do we need Jesus Christ? That question he answers in the first two and a half chapters. He points out, both to Jew and Gentile, what a mess they are in and how helpless and hopeless is their state.

Help and Hope

Not to fear. There is help and there is hope. Even if natural efforts as well as circumcision and the Law have proven bankrupt, there is no reason for despair. Your redeemer, your saviour, your help and hope is as close at hand as your yes in faith to Jesus Christ. He points out the way of faith beginning with Abraham, our father in faith, who showed that God holds open arms to us, not because we have been naturally good or behaved ourselves by obeying the Jewish Law, (which didn't exist in the time of Abraham), but because we have said "yes" to the Son and let him be Lord of our lives (Romans 4:16).

For Paul, the man without God is Adam. He is the counterpoint for Jesus Christ. Everything that he did wrong, sin, disobedience, death, is made up for by Jesus Christ. Adam turned the world upside down. Jesus turned it right side up. Beginning in chapter 5, Jesus is the new Adam, holy, obedient and life-giving. "Just as through one man's disobedience, all became sinners, so through one man's obedience, all became just" (5:19).

One of the problems about reading Paul's letter to the Romans is that so many have read it before us. Many grabbed a sentence out of context, didn't take Paul's total thought into consideration and carved one line into the stone of their own pre-conceived notions and beliefs.

Controversies

In the early Church, a group called the "Adoptionists" created a problem. For them, Jesus was a mere man, adopted as God's Son. They ripped out of context and used as their battle cry

Paul's loosely worded "he was made Son of God in power...by his resurrection from the dead" (1:3). Rather than recognizing that Paul meant here that Jesus was revealed as Son of God in power, they painted Paul's few words on a banner and went off to form their own Adoptionist Church.

Much later, Luther, rightly disgusted by the excesses and abuses of the Church in his time, zeroed in on "We hold that a person is justified by faith, apart from the Law" (3:28). Granted that Paul threw out the Law, he always insisted that we are accountable for our actions and will be rewarded or punished for them. He opted not just for faith, but "faith that works through love."

Calvin, having cornered the market on God's will, decided that some people were predestined to heaven, and others to hell. He chose for his bumper sticker the text: "God has mercy on whom he wishes, and whom he wishes he makes obdurate" (9:18). He ignores the fact that Paul prays for the obdurate (10:1) which would be futile if God's mind were already made up.

Not to be outdone, the Catholic Church at the Council of Trent (1545) defined the reality of original sin and the need for Baptism on the basis of Romans 5:12: "Therefore, just as through one man, sin entered the world and with sin, death, death thus coming to all men inasmuch as all sinned..." That's very true, but it was addressed to adult Christians, not to infants. As a matter of fact, the Church has never advocated the necessity of infant baptism to the extent that we should run through the nursery of a Jewish hospital, sprinkling water on all the infants. Baptism is only for those who have come to or are very likely to come

to adult, mature faith. Paul was no fool. He would not have baptized a child unless he were convinced that the faith of the parents would be handed on to it.

Death, Sin and Legalism

In chapters 6 and 7, Paul treats of the three enemies to our life in God through Jesus Christ: death, sin and Law. The first enemy, death, is vanquished by Baptism. In the early Church it was generally administered by going down into the water and rising out of it. The symbol of our identity with Jesus in his death and resurrection was very real. As

"Lord, you have made water holy through the baptism of Christ, that by the power of the Holy Spirit it may give your people a new birth" (Rite of Baptism).

"For I am convinced that neither death, nor life, nor angels, nor principalities, nor present things, nor future things, nor powers, nor height, nor depth, nor any other creature will be able to separate us from the love of God in Jesus Christ our Lord" (Romans 8:38-39).

the risen Lord conquered death, so did the Christian, rising from the waters of Baptism.

Since a dead person cannot sin, so in the death of Baptism, the cruel power of sin that lorded it over us is smashed. Because we have free will, we are still capable of sinning, but the Good News is that sin, as a controlling, domineering, despotic force in our lives, has been put in the same shackles with which it imprisoned us. "Sin will have power over you no longer, you are now under grace, and not under the Law" (6:14).

That brings Paul to the third element in this despotic triumvirate, the Law. Faith and Baptism have brought about a victory over all three. The dead cannot be punished for a violation of the law. They can respond neither to a parking ticket nor a summons. Law has no power over them. So too, the Mosaic Law has no binding force for the Christian who has died with Jesus, who has been made one in the Body of Christ: "You died to the Law through the Body of Christ, that you might belong to that other who was raised from the dead, so that we might bear fruit for God" (7:4).

At the end of chapter 7 (13-25), Paul paints a gruesome picture of himself (and all of us) without Christ. Without him we are helpless and hopeless. But Paul concludes with a resounding cry of help and hope: "What a wretched man I am! Who can free me from this body under the power of death? All praise to God, through Jesus Christ our Lord" (7:24).

Fulfillment in Hope

Chapter 8 is Paul at his best. It contains some of the most inspiring thoughts he wrote. He details the beauty of the Christian vocation. Redeemed by Christ we become free from sin, death and law. But that's only for starters. He sent the Holy Spirit to make us children of our Abba. Further, even this created universe joins us in yearning for the

PAUL AND THE HOLY SPIRIT

Paul never goes into deep theological discussion about the Holy Spirit. He just tells us what life in the Spirit is like:

1 Thessalonians 5:16, Do not stifle the Spirit.

Galatians 3:2, How did you receive the Spirit? Was it through observance of the law, or through faith in what you heard?

Galatians 6:22, The fruit of the Spirit is love, joy, peace, patient endurance, kindness, generosity, faith, mildness and chastity.... Since we live by the Spirit, let us follow the Spirit's lead.

1 Corinthians 12:3, No one can say Jesus is Lord except in the Holy Spirit.

1 Corinthians 12:7ff, To each person, the manifestation of the Spirit is given for the common good.... It is one and the same Spirit who produces all these gifts, distributing them to each at will.

Romans 8:14, All who are led by the Spirit of God are the children of God. You did not receive

a spirit of slavery leading you back into fear, but a spirit of adoption through which we cry out, "Abba" (that is, Father). The Spirit gives witness with our spirit that we are the children of God.

Romans 8:26, The Spirit, too, helps us in our weakness, for we do not know how to pray as we ought; but the Spirit makes intercession for us with groanings that cannot be expressed in speech.

2 Corinthians 1:21, God is the one who firmly establishes us along with you in Christ; it is God who anointed us and sealed us, thereby depositing the first payment, the Spirit in our hearts.

fullness of our salvation and redemption in Christ. There may still be troubles and distress, but they cannot overpower us: "We know that God makes all things work together for the good of those who have been called according to his decree" (8:28).

Our hope is indomitable for "if God is for us, who can be against us?" (8:31). He ends the chapter with an acclamation that declares every force that is against Jesus to be impotent: "I am certain that neither death nor life, neither angels nor principalities, neither the present nor the future, nor powers, neither height nor depth nor any other creature will be able to separate us from the love of God that comes to us in Christ Jesus, our Lord" (8:38).

Paul's Disappointment

Paul could have finished the letter with a magnificent flourish and ended here. Instead he must have eaten ice cream and pickles, had nightmares and woke up feeling sorry for himself. Then he took up the pen and put it all down on paper. Chapters 9, 10 and 11 spring from his bitter disappointment at his

failure to convert the entire Jewish people. The way he's been running around, it can't be his fault. If not his, then whose? It must be their own fault. But an entire nation can't be at fault, especially when they are the people whom God chose to make the divine plan known. If its neither of their faults, who is left. Only God! With some very loose language Paul implies that it is all in God's plan. He predestined some for salvation, others for perdition. Both you and I would cry out that it is not fair.

Paul anticipates the objection by giving the example of a potter who divides a lump of clay, making a piece of ceramic art out of half and a bowl for garbage out of the other. If they don't complain to the potter, who do we think we are, protesting God's decisions? It's a nice try, but it doesn't work. The figure fails. Lumps of clay don't have intellects and free will.

In the final analysis, Paul has confronted an insoluble puzzle. We know that God is all knowing, all powerful and the source of every grace. We are also aware that we have free will and are responsible for our actions. It is the permanent dilemma of grace and free will. Paul knows in his heart that his three chapters aren't going to resolve it. After all his argumentation, the last word is: "Oh, the depth of the riches and wisdom and knowledge of God! How inscrutable are God's judgments, how unsearchable are God's ways" (cf. 11:33). One could wish he had reached that conclusion three chapters earlier.

The remainder of Paul's letter to the Romans is largely a recapping of topics that he had written to the Corinthians about: the Body of Christ, proper use of charisms, the centrality of love, the exercise of one's "rights," and the living

out of the Christ life with a morality based on faith.

One section (13:1-7) is totally new, however. It concerns the relationship of the Christian to the civil authority. In a word, the government gets its authority from God, and is to be scrupulously obeyed. Paul has two reasons for canonizing the empire. First, the order and organization that it had imposed upon a barbaric world was a gift that helped in the spread of the Gospel, even to the speeding of his letters to their destinations. Secondly, he was on his way to the capitol of the empire where his own later martyrdom would show how the Christians were being considered disloyal, since they were claiming someone other than the emperor as Lord. Paul tried to clear the air, showing that a Christian could be a

good citizen. His martyrdom testifies that the Roman bureaucracy was not easily convinced.

As a matter of fact, since the Church always has to be prophetic to the culture and civilization in which it has taken root, Paul's lavish praise is turned to bitter condemnation in the next generation. Empire and emperor try to take the place of God. So the author of the Book of Revelation condemns the mistress of the world as the whore of Babylon. There's a good lesson for the Church today to remain loyal to the state by criticizing its false values.

"For the Reign of God is not a matter of food and drink, but of righteousness, peace and joy in the Holy Spirit....Let us then pursue what leads to peace and to building up one another" (Romans 14;17,190).

10

LETTERS TO THE EPHESIANS AND THE COLOSSIANS

One would not think time spent in jail to be among the most productive times of one's life. For Paul it was just that. The reason why these two magnificent and insightful letters are called "Captivity Epistles" is that it was thought that they were written by Paul while he was in jail. Even chains and bars could not stifle the Good News.

Admittedly, he is not the founder or evangelizer of these communities. He has, however, heard of some of the problems

Jesus is the heartbeat of the universe, the center of spiritual gravity in the cosmos.

They were in charge of the various aspects and areas of the life of us poor mortals. Living a peaceful life meant keeping those heavenly powers satisfied and placated. To get on the wrong side of them meant trouble. They believed strongly in this system but just were not sure where Jesus fit into it. What was his area of specialization?

Intervening Powers

This was a challenge for the author. Jesus was indeed a specialist in the salvation and redemption of all peoples. But what was Jesus' relationship to the entire created world, the cosmos, the invisible principalities or powers? Paul's reply is that Jesus does not fit into the picture, he is the picture. He doesn't fit into our system, he is the system. He is the heartbeat of the universe, the center of spiritual gravity in the cosmos.

If a man is drowning, he doesn't ask his rescuer what he does for a living. He desperately reaches out for help. Before his conversion, Paul was drowning in the Law. He rejoiced at his salvation in Christ. In Romans he was preoccupied with showing how Jesus saved us from the Law, sin and death. In a sense he never asked what Jesus did for a living. That means asking not just what is his relationship to drowning people, it means asking about the big picture. The Ephesians and Colossians have forced him to ask where Jesus fits into the whole picture. His answer is one of the most profound of the entire Bible:

they have been facing. He feels a compulsion to show them how his own deepening understanding of the role of Jesus will help them overcome those problems.

The principal tension arose because of their previous beliefs. They wanted to hold on to them and wondered just where Jesus fit into the picture. They believed in one God. They also believed that, between themselves and that God in the invisible heavenly world, there were numerous intermediating gods, each one of whom was a specialist.

> He is the image of the invisible God, the first-born of all creatures. In him everything in heaven and on earth was created, things visible and invisible, whether thrones or dominations, principalities or

powers; all were created through him, and for him. He is before all else that is. In him everything continues in being. It is he who is head of the Body, the Church; he who is the beginning, the first-born of the dead, so that primacy may be his in everything. It pleased God to make absolute fullness reside in him and, by means of him, to reconcile everything in his person, both on earth and in the heavens, making peace through the blood of his cross (Colossians 1:15-20).

Jesus at Home

To put it quite plainly, the vision that Paul arrives at late in his life is that Jesus came into this world not as a stranger, but to his home. He is not an afterthought in the plan of God, nor a footnote in salvation history. There is absolutely nothing in this entire universe that was not made for him, including Adam. The sixfold chorus of "all things" admits of no exception. That is why one of the early church writers could exclaim, "O soul that is naturally Christian." Everyone who ever was, is, or will be was made for the sake of Jesus Christ. There are no exceptions, only those who haven't heard about it yet.

The author puts this fascinating revelation in another way in Ephesians:

Praised be the God and Father of our Lord Jesus Christ, who has bestowed on us in Christ every spiritual blessing in the heavens! God chose us in him before the world began, to be holy and blameless in his sight, to be full of love; God likewise predestined us through Christ Jesus to be his adopted children - such was his will and pleasure - that all might praise the glorious favor bestowed on us in God's beloved (Colossians 1:3-6).

Think of it! Before the world was created, Jesus Christ was already in the

plan of God. God didn't create the world and then decide to send his son. God planned the incarnation of his divine Son and then planned the world as a home for him.

And before God said in Genesis, "Let there be light," God's eye was already on us to be children of light, God's very own sons and daughters, the brothers and sisters of Jesus. He is not an afterthought and neither are we.

This may be difficult to comprehend because we usually think chronologically. First came creation, then came Adam, then Jesus, and finally ourselves. Paul, however, would have us lift our eyes from the calendar of history to the meaning and plan of history in the mind of God:

In all wisdom and insight, God has made known to us the mystery of his will in accord with his favor that he set forth in him as a plan for the fullness of times, to sum up all things in Christ, in heaven and on earth (Ephesians 1:8-10).

Some translations say: "to restore all things in Christ," or "to recapitulate all things in Christ (1:9-10). However it is expressed, what is meant is that God's plan is to gather together once again

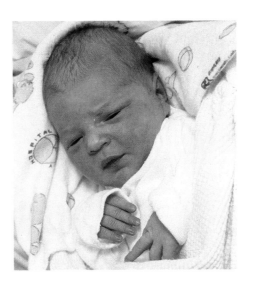

And before God said in Genesis, "Let there be light," God's eye was already on us to be children of light, God's very own sons and daughters, the brothers and sisters of Jesus. He is not an afterthought and neither are we.

every creature of the universe, putting creation back where it belongs, oriented to Jesus Christ.

Examining a plan of your own may help you understand God's plan, centered in Jesus Christ. If you plan on a trip to Europe, the last thing to happen is the arrival in Europe, though it is the first thing on your mind. First comes packing, guide books, buying tickets, boarding the plane, and later comes the arrival. So with God, if Jesus seems to have arrived late on the scene, it was still the fullness of time, for he was central to the plan of his Father.

Christocentric Creation

This sheds a whole new light on all of creation. It is christocentric. If we could interpret the song of the bird, the roaring of the wave, the whistling of the breeze or the patter of the rain, we would hear them singing in chorus: "We were made for Jesus Christ." No wonder that a Francis of Assisi, who so perfectly entered into and lived God's plan, could sing of Brother Sun and Sister Moon.

Jesus came to put things back in their place, to restore all things to himself.

ST. FRANCIS' CANTICLE OF THE CREATURES

Be praised, my Lord, in all your creatures,
especially Brother Sun
who makes daytime,
and through him you give us light.
And he is beautiful, radiant with great splendor,
and he is a sign
that tells, All-highest, of you.

Be praised, my Lord, for Sister Moon and the stars;
you formed them in the sky,
bright and precious and beautiful.

Be praised, my Lord, for Brother Wind,
and for the air and the clouds,
and for fair, and every kind of weather,
by which you give your creatures food.

Be praised, my Lord, for Sister Water,
who is most useful and humble
and lovely and chaste.

Be praised, my Lord, for Brother Fire,
through whom you light up the night for us;

and he is beautiful and jolly
and lusty and strong.
Be praised, my Lord, for our Sister Mother Earth,
who keeps us and feeds us
and brings forth fruits of many kinds,
with colored flowers and plants as well.

We continue God's plan when we touch God's people and God's creation with love. We point them in the right direction, the way they should be going, toward Jesus Christ.

For Paul, this mission of the primacy of Jesus Christ is not subtle theological speculation. It is the very stuff of our existence, and he prayed that it would be realized in us:

> That is why I kneel before the Father from whom every family in heaven and on earth takes its name; and I pray that he will bestow on you gifts in keeping

with the riches of his glory. May he strengthen you inwardly through the working of his Spirit. May Christ dwell in your hearts through faith, and may charity be the root and foundation of your life. Thus you will be able to grasp fully, with all the holy ones, the breadth and length and height and depth of Christ's love, and experience this love which surpasses all knowledge, so that you may attain to the fullness of God himself. To him whose power now at work in us can do immeasurably more than we ask or imagine - to him be glory in the Church and in Christ Jesus through all generations, world without end. Amen (Ephesians 3:14-21).

"May Christ dwell in your hearts through faith, and may charity be the root and foundation of your life. That you will be able to grasp fully, with all the holy ones, the breadth and length and heig:'th and depth of Christ's love, and experience this love which surpasses all understanding"
(Ephesians 3:14-21).

11

PASTORAL LETTERS

LETTERS TO TIMOTHY

Imagine having the rare opportunity to be able to tell a bishop how he is to behave and how he is to run his Church. That's what the letters to Timothy and Titus do. Apparently Timothy had the care of the community at Ephesus which was also the destination of the letter to the Ephesians, and the critical letter in the Book of Revelation: "I hold this against you: You have turned aside from your early love. Keep firmly in mind the heights from which you have fallen, and return to your former deeds" (Revelation 2:4).

102

"The Church has a visible social structure, which is a sign of its unity in Christ..." (Vatican Council II, 1965).

If their ardor and enthusiasm has waned, their faithfulness to correct teaching has not: "You have tested those self-styled apostles, who are nothing of the sort, and discovered that they are imposters" (Revelation 2:2).

The letters to Timothy reflect some of the turmoil caused by those "self-styled apostles." To those who want to return to religion by Law he writes:

> The Law is aimed not at good people, but at the lawless and unruly, the irreligious and sinful, the wicked and the godless, those who kill their fathers and mothers, murderers, fornicators, sexual perverts, kidnappers, liars, perjurers, and those who in other ways flout the sound teaching that pertains to the glorious Gospel of God (1 Timothy 1:9 ff).

The next time people yearn for the good old days of law, ask them in which category they fit!

Also identified are some "plausible liars...who forbid marriage and require abstinence from foods which God created to be received with thanksgiving by believers who know the truth" (1 Timothy 4:3). In a note of care and concern, he emphasizes that all food

(and drink!) is a gift from God. The author tells Timothy: "Stop drinking water only. Take a little wine for the good of your stomach and because of your frequent illness" (5:23).

Both letters to Timothy are filled with warnings to fidelity, advice on the proper running of the Church, as well as homey advice.

TITUS

The letter to Titus, charged with the care of the community on the island of Crete, continues the themes of pastoral solicitude, but with some rather harsh words for the Cretans: "There are many irresponsible teachers, especially from among the Jewish converts, who are empty talkers and deceivers" (1:10). Fair enough. The author knows that from experience, but he gets a bit carried away when he quotes from one of their own writers: "Cretans have ever been liars, beasts and lazy gluttons" (1:12). That's not exactly how to win friends and influence people, and one can only hope that Titus never read this letter to his parishioners.

If he did share part of the letter, hopefully it was the digest version of the Gospel in Titus 2:11-14:

> The grace of God has appeared, offering salvation to all people. It trains us to reject godless ways and worldly desires, and live temperately, justly, and devoutly in this age as we await our blessed hope, the appearing of the glory of the great God and of our Savior Christ Jesus. It was he who sacrificed himself for us, to redeem us from all unrighteousness and to cleanse for himself a people of his own, eager to do what is right.

PHILEMON

This is a letter to a Christian slave owner about his runaway slave who is now also his brother. He, too, has been converted by Paul and become a Christian. The shortest book of the Bible, it is touching in Paul's concern for both slave and master.

Obviously, neither Philemon nor Paul had any question or the slightest doubt about the morality of slavery. In 1 Corinthians 7:21 Paul goes so far as to say,

> Were you a slave when you were called (to the faith)? Give it no thought. Even supposing you could go free, you would be better off making the most of your slavery.... Each of you should continue before God in the condition of life that was his when he was called.

Paul thought that relationship to Jesus Christ eclipsed every other relationship. He was just accepting the given social structure of the empire. Still, how can it be that what we consider the height of immorality today was neither questioned by the early Christians, nor prohibited by the commandments? Today we are dismayed at the very thought of one person enslaving another.

Obviously, our sense of what is moral and immoral has changed and developed. The New Testament is a good starting point for the study of morality, but it is not the last word.

HEBREWS

Ecumenical meetings between Protestants and Catholics are meant to clear the air. Too often we have presumed we knew what others believed before even listening to them.

At a recent meeting, the Catholic belief of Mass as a sacrifice was being discussed. The Protestant parties said that they were dismayed by such belief since it was so contrary to the Bible. They quoted the New Testament book of Hebrews, the only New Testament document to call Jesus a priest; and

"The Reign of God is of everybody and for everybody. God's Reign is offered in a special way to the poor, not because they are better, but rather because for them the coming of God's Reign is especially good news" (Segundo Galilea).

QUMRAN

In 1947 a shepherd boy discovered caves in the wilderness near the Dead Sea. Inside were scrolls hidden by people called Essenes, a sect of Judaism. As the Roman army advanced in 68 A.D. the members hid their precious library, expecting to return for it in a few weeks. A Roman garrison occupied their buildings, preventing their return.

Copies of almost every book of the Bible as well as some Essene books have been recovered. They tell us a great deal about this community that was contemporaneous with the rise of Christianity and in some ways similar to it.

They had a martyred leader called the "Teacher of Righteousness." They, too, considered themselves the true Israel waiting impatiently for the end times. While waiting, they too lived a communal life not unlike the Jerusalem community that Luke describes in Acts. They had initiation rites and ritual meals. They were looking for not one messiah, but two, modeled upon David and Aaron.

There were also great dissimilarities. Their warrior messiah (David) was the same as what other Jews expected. Jesus refused to be that. Again, they were scrupulously minute in legal observance, whereas Jesus said that the sabbath was made for people and not people for the sabbath (Mark 2:27). The Essenes of Qumran not only avoided everyone outside the community, they considered them hated enemies. Jesus associated with prostitutes and sinners and said, "Love your enemies." They separated themselves totally from the world. Jesus told his disciples to convert it.

Besides their gift to us of the ancient biblical texts, have the Essenes left any other inheritance to Christianity? Did they influence it in any way? Not enough research has been done to know for certain, but it would be a bit surprising if they

haven't. John the Baptist preached in the wilderness where they lived. In going up from Jericho to Jerusalem, Jesus passed nearby. Whether or not he or John or their disciples had contact with the Essene community remains at present a moot question.

Could some of the Essenes have become converts to Christianity after they fled the Romans? One of their scrolls, the Damascus Document, found in Egypt, indicates that they were widely dispersed. It is not at all unlikely that they recognized an affinity with Christianity and embraced it without giving up their previous narrow, sectarian beliefs, which they may have tried to impose on their Christian community. There is a clue in the strange insertion made in 2 Corinthians 6:14-7:1. Paul never used the term "Belial" of the devil. The Essenes of Qumran always referred to the devil as Belial!

without a priest sacrifice is impossible. Their argument: Jesus sacrificed once, and then:

> He entered heaven itself that he might appear before God on our behalf. Not that he might offer himself there again and again...if that were so, he would have had to suffer death over and over from the creation of the world. But now he has appeared at the end of the ages to take away sins once for all by his sacrifice. Just as it is appointed that people die once,...so Christ was offered up once to take away the sins of many (Hebrews 9:24 ff).

> We have been sanctified through the offering of the Body of Jesus Christ once for all.... Jesus offered one sacrifice for sins and took his seat at the right hand of God.... By one offering he has forever perfected those who are being sanctified (10:10 ff).

Transforming Sacrifice

The Mass is at the very heart of Catholic life and belief. The Vatican Council called it the summit and source of the Church's activity.

Here was the dilemma: If the Mass is a repetition of the sacrifice of Calvary, it implies that Jesus did not do his job. His sacrifice was incomplete if it has to be repeated. The dilemma was resolved with an insight from modern biblical scholarship. It gave a deeper, fuller and more complete understanding of what sacrifice is, and what priesthood is.

Most people think of sacrifice as the destruction of a victim. That's why they are turned off by the Old Testament and its implied image of God. God seems to be an ogre, kept happy and placated by the destruction of as many "victims" as possible. It is just too bloody.

That is a misunderstanding of sacrifice. Sacrifice is not the destruction, but the transformation of a victim. For the Israelites, life was blood and blood was life. By the pouring out of its blood, the victim was being transformed into a new state of existence dedicated to God. The transformation of the victim stood for and symbolized the transformation that the offerer was willing to undergo in living out more deeply a life with God. God didn't want dead animals, but live people. They were only truly alive when they lived in God as was signified in pouring out the blood and transforming the life of the individual.

Many people had a confused idea even of lenten sacrifices. They were good because they hurt. Not at all. They were good when they transformed us to live a more vibrant life with the Lord on Easter Sunday.

Transformation is the key. If we apply that to the sacrifice of Jesus, it opens the door to the meaning of sacrifice. He is the victim. His sacrifice does not

"Christ taught us that human dignity is to be found in loving. For God, this dignity and the human freedom to love or not to love is what comes first....God loves human beings so much that God bets on us and then totally respects us" (Segundo Galilea).

"Jesus Christ...gave himself for us to deliver us from all lawlessness and to cleanse for himself a people as his own, eager to do what is good" (Titus 2:13-14).

consist in his death or destruction. No, it is in his transformation, dead, risen and glorified. It is what John, in his Gospel calls the "Hour" of Jesus. We can date the beginning of his sacrifice: three o'clock, Good Friday afternoon. We cannot date its end. In resurrection he went from time into eternity where there are no watches, clocks, or calendars. His sacrifice is not over. It continues. It is still going on in eternity.

The Protestants were correct in quoting the "once and for all" about the sacrifice of Jesus. The Catholics are also correct, although they had been using imprecise language. The Mass is a sacrifice, not because it repeats the sacrifice of Calvary. His death there was only the beginning of his sacrifice, not the end. It has not ended. It continues in eternity, and breaks into time in the Mass. In the Liturgy we do not repeat the past, we make present the eternal and ongoing sacrifice of Jesus.

At the ecumenical meeting the Protestants agreed that in light of this, the Mass could indeed be a sacrifice. Hebrews, the very document that they had quoted, insists that the work of Jesus is still going on in eternity:

Fix your eyes on Jesus, the apostle and high priest whom we acknowledge in faith (3:1). For we do not have a high priest who is unable to sympathize with our weakness.... So let us confidently approach the throne of grace to receive mercy and favor and to find help in time of need (4:16).

When perfected (i.e., consecrated, not destroyed) he became the source of eternal salvation for all who obey him (5:9).

Jesus, our forerunner has entered (heaven) on our behalf, being made high priest forever according to the order of Melchizedek (6:20).

Unlike the other high priests, he has no need to offer sacrifice day after day;...he did that once for all when he offered himself (7:27).

Two things are essential for sacrifice. Priest (or offerer) and victim. Jesus is both in his sacrifice. But when Jesus was on the cross there were men crucified on either side of him. They all met the same fate. What made his a sacrifice and theirs a tragedy? In Jerusalem many animals were slaughtered in the markets, some were sacrificed in the temple. What makes the difference? The answer: the attitude of the priest offerer. Slaughter is transformed into sacrifice by the attitude of the one offering. Without love and petition for union with God, there is only tragedy and slaughter.

It is the love and prayer with which Jesus offers himself that continues in heaven. "He is our advocate who always pleads our cause." If his sacrifice is not over and done with, then neither is his priesthood:

He entered heaven itself that he might appear before God now on our behalf (9:24). He had to become like his sisters and brothers in every way, that he might be a merciful and faithful high priest on their behalf, to expiate the sins of the people (3:17). He is always able to save those who approach God through him, since he forever lives to make intercession for them (7:25). We have, in the presence of the Father, Jesus Christ, an intercessor who is just! (1 John 2:1).

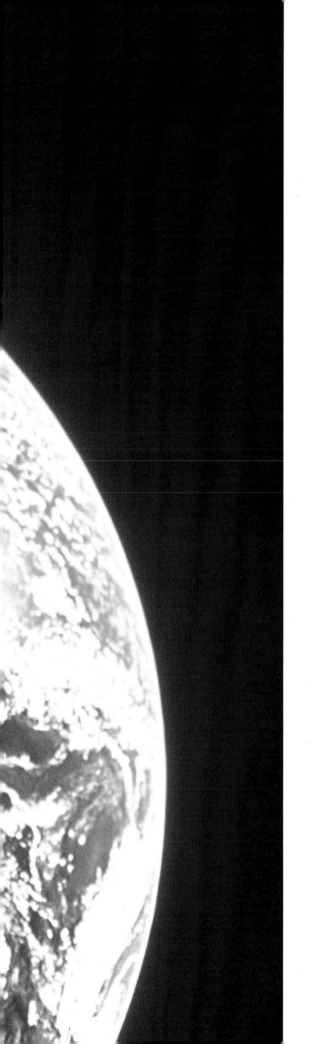

12

THE CATHOLIC EPISTLES

S even short New Testament letters
are called "catholic." That
does not refer to the religion of their authors.
They are catholic with a small "c" which
means "universal." The letters from James,
Peter, John, and Jude are given that
designation because they are not addressed to
individual Churches, but to the Church
universal.

JAMES

The letter of James gained notoriety at the time of the Reformation when Luther dubbed it the "straw epistle." He was preoccupied with the role of faith and therefore was unhappy with James' emphasis on works. "What good is it to profess faith without practicing it? Such faith has no power to save one, has it?... Faith without good works is dead" (James 2:14 ff). Obviously the author has met "Christians" who think that religion is a private affair and that expressions of faith are best saved for Sunday morning in church. Luther misunderstood James. James is not proposing that we can earn our salvation by the works we do. He is saying that faith is not a matter of lips professing a creed. James says that the vibrant quality of one's faith can be

measured by one's activity. "By their fruits you shall know them" (Matthew 12:33).

1 PETER

The first letter of Peter may have had its origin in a baptismal liturgy or a ceremony similar to the new Rite of Christian Initiation for Adults (RCIA), recently introduced into the Church. The letter starts out by giving thanks for the "new birth" which draws its hope from the risen Lord. "Although you have never seen him, you love him, and without seeing, you now believe in him and rejoice with inexpressible joy, touched with glory, because you are achieving faith's goal, your salvation" (1:8).

LETTERS TO THE CHURCHES

What is the Church? Paul's letters are addressed each to a Church. But if Paul rang your doorbell today and asked you to take him to the Church, where would you take him? If you took him to Sacred Heart, St. Anthony or Our Lady of Lourdes, he would collapse laughing. In his wildest dreams, he could never imagine anyone confusing a building with the Church.

Paul and all the New Testament writers had many synonyms for Church. The only time it is called a building is when we, the members, are described as the building material and Jesus Christ is the corner stone (Ephesians 2:19).

Long before "Holy Communion" was used to refer to a sacrament, it defined Church. "Communion" is one of Paul's and John's favorite words to designate the Church. (It is sometimes

translated as fellowship). But it is when we are called the Body of Christ that Paul most vividly challenges us to an awareness of what Jesus has accomplished in us. As surely as the Eucharist is, so are we the Body of Christ. In him, you and I are as closely related as my hand is to my arm.

"If a brother or sister has nothing to wear and no food for the day, and one of you says to them, 'Go in peace, keep warm, and eat well,' but you do not give them the necessities of the body, what good is it? So also faith itself, if it does not have works, is dead" *(James 2:15-17).*

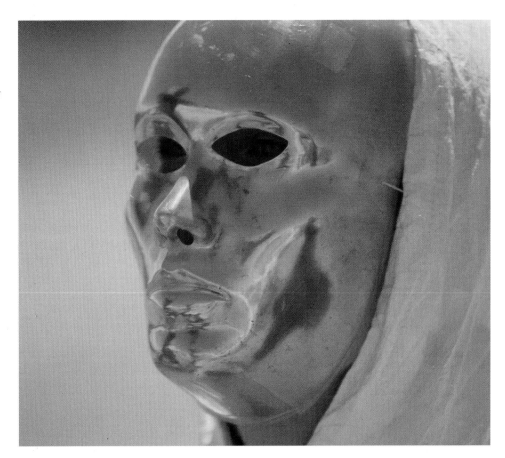

2 PETER

The second letter of Peter was probably the last book of the New Testament to be written. It is concerned with false teachers in the community. Their version of Christianity is more akin to an orgy than to a religion:

> These people pour abuse on things of which they are ignorant.... Thinking daytime revelry a delight, they are a stain and a defilement as they share your feasts in a spirit of seduction. Constantly on the lookout for a sexual partner, theirs is a never ending search for sin. They lure the weaker types. They talk empty bombast, while baiting their hooks with passion, with the lustful ways of the flesh, to catch those who have just come free of a life of errors. They promise them freedom, though they themselves are slaves of corruption (2 Peter 2:12 ff).

That's not a pretty picture of those who were using religion as a mask for pleasure and gain.

1 JOHN

1 John is written to confront a different problem. It is the problem of the anti-Christ. This is the only New Testament document to mention this evil figure. John's description of him is a far cry from what modern fundamentalist preachers have made him out to be: "Just as you heard that the antichrist was coming, so now many such antichrists have appeared.... It was from our ranks that they took their leave" (1 John 2:18). Later, he specifies just what is the problem with these mischief-making apostates:

Every spirit that acknowledges Jesus Christ come in the flesh belongs to God, while every spirit that fails to acknowledge him does not belong to God. Such is the spirit of the antichrist which, as you have heard, is to come; in fact, it is in the world already (4:2).

Denial of the humanity of Jesus was the creed of the antichrists. They were Docetists who could not accept that "The Word was made flesh." They made Jesus into an apparition. Serious business, for if he was not one of us, then he did not redeem us. "He had to become like us in every way, that he might be a merciful and faithful high priest before God on our behalf" (Hebrews 2:17).

2 & 3 JOHN

The second letter of John is still preoccupied with this problem. "Many deceitful men have gone out into the world, men who do not acknowledge Jesus Christ as coming in the flesh" (7). The third letter shows that the Church is settling in nicely. It is a plea for the support of the clergy!

JUDE

Jude's letter deals with the same problem as 1 Peter:

> Certain individuals have recently wormed their way into your midst, godless types, long ago destined for the condemnation I shall describe. They pervert the gracious gift of our God to sexual excess and deny Jesus Christ, our only master and Lord (4).

Although short in length these "catholic" epistles manifest the Spirit at work in the early Church as it struggled to find its identity, by identifying those who were perverting the Gospel.

"And the victory that conquers the world is our faith. Who [indeed] is the victor over the world but the one who believes that Jesus is the Son of God" (1 John 5:4-5)?

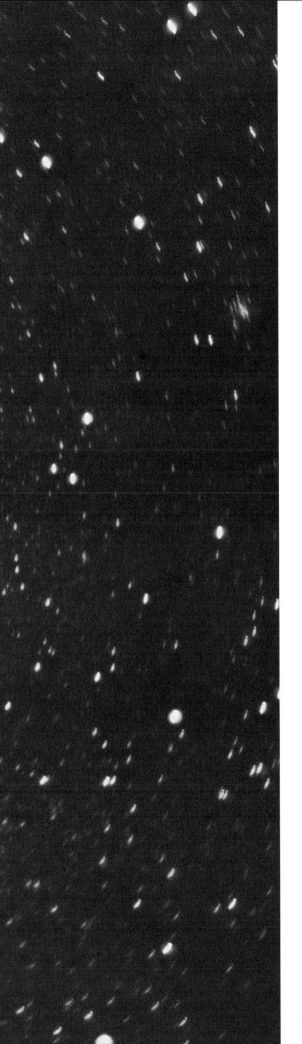

13

THE BOOK OF REVELATION

INTRODUCTION TO
APOCALYPTIC LITERATURE

Have you checked your mail today? If so, you probably received all different kinds of literature. Some you can recognize by the envelope and decide which ones go into the circular file, unopened. Depending on the time of year there may be appeals for your vote and/or wallet from political candidates. There may be catalogues, charitable appeals, newsletters, magazines, sale notices, and if you are lucky, even invitations, thank you notes or letters from friends. There is a category for each piece

When the world situation seems to be verging on chaos and God seems to have taken an early vacation, then apocalypses appear in mail boxes and on news stands. Such is the Book of Revelation with its beautiful message: God is alive and well and in charge!

of mail, and very often you know what to expect before you open it.

Unless you have fallen prey to the computerized mailing list of a fundamentalist TV evangelist, you probably won't receive anything like an apocalyptic style letter. But when the Churches of Asia Minor opened the mail from the prison colony on Patmos they found an apocalypse. They didn't even have to guess what it was all about. They were familiar with the symbolic category and type of literature it fit into. So that there would be no

possible chance of a mistake, however, the author lets the cat out of the bag in the first line: "This is the Apocalypse of Jesus Christ."

The word means "revelation." It belongs to a class of literature that was common just before and after the coming of Jesus. It was the heir of prophetic literature which was meant to comfort the afflicted and afflict the comfortable. The purpose of apocalyptic literature was the same, but with this difference: It emerges on the scene when the world situation seems to be verging on chaos. When peace has been shattered, the forces of evil seem to be triumphing, the community feels abandoned to the powers of darkness, and God seems to have taken early retirement, then apocalypses appear in mail boxes and on news stands. They have rightly been called tracts for hard times.

Since the time of Emperor Nero (65 A.D.) the peace of the Roman Empire had been shattered. Paul's own martyrdom was proof that the situation had worsened. Nero had the reputation of throwing lavish parties illuminated by the flaming bodies of oil drenched Christians. Things hit bottom in the mid-nineties when "divine" Diocletian declared himself to be a god and demanded worship as proof of loyalty to the empire. Failure to worship meant torture, exile, imprisonment or death. The author of Revelation was already exiled to the penal colony of Patmos for having taken a stand. He had decided who is Lord. He wrote this book to help his fellow Christians in making their decision.

This apocalyptic letter doesn't predict the future, it gives hope for the present. The author lets the community know that, all appearances to the contrary,

God is in charge and Jesus is Lord. Revelation is an invitation to renewed faith and enduring hope.

Evidence of the desperation of these suffering Christians can be seen in 6:10 where the martyrs cry out to God to avenge their blood. That's not quite what Jesus said about turning the other cheek. And then it looks like the author has God playing games when God says he'll get around to the vengeance as soon as the quota of those to be slain is filled. This is the exaggerated and imprecise language of a Church beside itself because of terrible suffering and demented persecution. Such hyperbole should not blind us to the beautiful message of the Book of Revelation: God is alive and well and in charge. "He's got the whole world in his hands!"

Symbol or Reality?

Some Christians take the Bible for granted. Others ignore it. But the worst aberration is that of Christians who act as if Revelation is the only book that God wrote. In addition to ripping it out of the total context of God's Word contained in the Bible, they treat it as if its literary form were that of the itinerary drawn up by the divine travel agent with the final destination as the last judgment. They cheer and rejoice at every calamity, disaster and war because they see these as intermediate stepping stones leading to better things to come. The worse the events are, the more likely the end is at hand.

They confuse the symbol with the reality and miss the point that the inspired author, and therefore God, was trying to make. If anything is clear from the entire Bible, it is that God does not give sneak previews. God's Word is

always meant to challenge in the present, not give security or certainty for the future.

Since the Book of Revelation has been co-opted by certain fundamentalist Churches, many Christians have gladly abandoned it to their clutches and all but ignored it. That is too bad, for behind the language, imagery and symbol there is a powerful message for the Church.

It is a message that challenges us to look forward in hope, knowing that God is almighty and Jesus is Lord. This is portrayed in the symbolism of the vision of Jesus in the first chapter. Each symbolic element tells us something about him. The sash of gold signifies his kingship, the white hair, his wisdom, the blazing eyes tell us that he sees what's going on. The feet of brass speak of his strength and constancy. His roaring voice tells of the power of his Word. The stage is set. The last

The woman clothed with the sun has multiple symbolism. She may be interpreted as Eve or Israel; or for the early Christians, Mary the mother of Jesus and mother of the Church.

CHARACTERISTICS OF APOCALYPTIC LITERATURE

Each kind of literature is unique and has its own traits and characteristics. Failure to recognize these differences leads to a misunderstanding of the message. Important characteristics of apocalyptic literature are:

1. AUTHOR UNKNOWN: Apocalyptic literature is generally written under a pseudonym. Authors must protect their identities since they are advocating open rebellion against the anti-God forces, often the state. Usually the authors borrow the name of a famous person who is deceased.

2. ANTIQUARIANISM: When the prophets gave their rare descriptions of the future they did it in terms of the good old days: Paradise, exodus, Abraham, Moses, David, etc. Apocalyptic authors describe their present situation in terms of the bad old days: chaos, plagues, disaster, the beast of chaos, prominent in some creation accounts, etc.

3. SYMBOLISM: It is essential to apocalyptic writing. It closes the door to the real meaning unless you have the keys. The authors are familiar with the Old Testament (two-thirds of Revelation is made up of quotes from it). They also have faith that the present distress is merely a prelude to the Reign of God. Lacking these, the enemies described in Revelation don't recognize themselves, believing that the weird symbolism is the work of an unbalanced mind.

4. NUMEROLOGY - The ancient languages had no numbers, so they employed the alphabet to count (cf. the Roman numerals MCXVI, etc.).

Thus every word had a numerical value (cf. Matthew's genealogy where David is number fourteen) and groups of numbers could conceal a word (cf. 666 of Revelation 13:18). Certain numbers also have meaning. Twelve is the number of God's people (from the patriarchs or apostles). Seven is the lucky number of perfection, and six is an imposter since it falls short of seven. Four is cosmic, universal from the points of the compass. One thousand and its multiples refer to what is infinite and uncountable.

5. FUTURE ORIENTED: To throw powerful enemies off the track, the author pretends to speak about what will happen in the future. The intolerable conditions of the time are really what is being described. It is not a preview of coming attractions. In this description, the readers recognized their own situation. There is only one thing said about the future: God will not be mocked and God's day will come!

word has already been said. It is Jesus. No matter what else follows, no power in heaven or earth can overcome him. We know that he is already what he will be proclaimed at the end of the book: "King of Kings and Lord of Lords" (19:16).

Examination of Conscience

With the stage thus set with Jesus arrayed as conquerer, we would expect to get right into the fray, for the community has already pointed its finger at the enemy. But the author now implies that the finger may be pointed in the wrong direction. If you have ever dealt with alcoholics, you know they can easily point the finger at others as the cause of their problems. Until they point the finger at themselves, they will not be on the road to recovery. The author indicates that the same is true of us. We so easily point the finger at God's enemies: godless atheism, communism, foreigners, non-Catholics, etc.

It is so easy to finger one of these typical "enemies" and avoid realizing that God's worst enemies are smug, complacent, mediocre, lukewarm Christians. That is why, before writing a diatribe against the Roman Empire, the author writes an examination of conscience for the Churches. They have lost their first fervor, left their first love. They have compromised the faith for the sake of security and fear of persecution. They have watered down their commitment. The accusation against Laodicea sums it all up: "You are neither cold nor hot. I wish you were either cold or hot! So, because you are lukewarm, neither hot nor cold, I will spit you out of my mouth" (3:15). The author would have been

delighted with a recent poster that asks: "If you were arrested for being a Christian, would there be enough evidence to convict you?"

Creation out of Chaos

In chapters 4 and 5 the author takes his readers to church. He lifts back the veil to show them the heavenly liturgy. What a vision for the readers, who could have been arrested for worshipping together! If they could not publicly participate in the earthly liturgy, they could at least contemplate the heavenly one.

"God is so different from us, and our intelligence is so limited before God, that we are dazzled when God communicates divine truths to us....Too much light blinds us. That is why we need faith to receive the Light" (Segundo Galilea).

Borrowing from the prophet Zechariah, also an apocalyptic writer, the author now introduces the four horsemen with their plagues, tragedies and disasters. The world seems to be returning to chaos. No problem. God can bring creation out of chaos again.

144,000?

Chapter 7 is the favorite one of the Jehovah's Witnesses. They insist that the number 144,000 be taken absolutely literally and that only these are going to heaven, and you can be sure they will all be Jehovah's Witnesses! Some time ago one of them was challenged on this literal interpretation of one number when the book is so full of numbers and other symbols. He adamantly insisted that not one more or less than

144,000 would be in heaven. When it was pointed out that according to the author's mentality it was symbolic of an infinite uncountable number (cf. 7:9: "A huge crowd which no one could count"), he stuck to his guns.

Then it was pointed out to him that a few verses later the crowd is said to worship the Lamb. Did he think that when he got to heaven, he would prostrate himself before a little wooly lamb? He changed his tune and said that while 144,000 was literal, the lamb was symbolic. As strange as it may be, the Book of Revelation is not as strange as some of its interpreters.

Dragons and Beasts

The singing eagle of 13:8 with its lament of "Woe, woe and again woe," sums up the next few chapters as the author depicts chaos apparently reclaiming God's creation. (It is only "apparent" for we already know the last chapter of this mystery.)

Woes and sorrows give way to dragons and beasts in chapters 12 and 13. In the ancient world they are symbolic of evil and chaos and every one or thing that rears its head against the Almighty. In early parts of the Bible such beasts even found their way in as that prime matter which God slaughtered to make creation (cf. Isaiah 27:1, Job 26:12, Psalm 74:13).

The Woman

The woman clothed with the sun (12:1) has a multiple symbolism. It is not known exactly which or how many meanings the original author intended to include. This woman may refer to Eve, the mother of humanity (Genesis 3:15-20), since the dragon is said to stand for "the ancient serpent, known as the devil or Satan, the seducer of the whole world" (12:9). He makes war on her anointed son and "on the rest of her offspring" (12:17). The woman clothed in the sun may also signify the whole people of Israel in which case the twelve stars symbolize the twelve tribes. Again, the author may be pointing to the remnant that faithfully awaits the Messiah (Isaiah 66:7). Finally, early Christians would include Mary, the mother of Jesus in this symbol, or Mary, the mother of the disciples (John 19:25-27), or the mother of the new people of God, the Church (12 stars = 12 apostles).

666?

In chapter 13 two beasts emerge on the scene. One stands for the Roman Empire with all its oppressive bureaucracy and power which is now under the control of the dragon, already identified as Satan. The dragon is the scourge of God's people who suffer bitterly under its oppression. The second beast is the great enigma of history. "A certain wisdom is needed here; with a little ingenuity anyone can calculate the number of the beast for it is a number that stands for a certain man. The man's number is 666" (13:18).

A little ingenuity has gone a long way. Throughout history those who interpret the Bible literally have branded their real or supposed enemy with 666. It has been applied to everyone from the Pope to the Internal Revenue Service.

Obviously the author had someone of his own generation in mind. The letters for Emperor Nero do add up to 666. But since the woman clothed with the sun had several meanings, the same may be true here. It may stand for Nero who began the bloody persecution or Diocletian, the despotic emperor at the time of writing. He did put to death any who refused to worship his image (13:15 ff).

But the author may have had something further in mind. A few lines later (17:14) he proclaims that Jesus is Lord of Lords and King of Kings. The numerical equivalent of those letters add up to 777. That is the number of fullness, perfection and power. Then 666 is the designation of that which falls short of 777 and tries to usurp its power. 666 then is every force that tries to take the place of Jesus and will not

"This is the fountain of life, water made holy by the suffering of Christ, washing all the world. You who are washed in this water have hope of life eternal" (Ancient Baptismal Liturgy)

allow him to be Lord, or accept his dominion. There may be a little of 666 in each one of us.

Interpretation Key

Chapter 17 is the clue to the interpretation of the whole book. Revelation is not concerned with predicting the future, but uncovering the source of present (96 A.D.) evils, Rome, the "whore of Babylon."

The author knows from history that empires have come and gone, but the power of the Lord endures forever. Babylon, the great enemy of God's people in the Old Testament, exists no more. He has no doubt that the same fate awaits the present tyrant and borrows the language of Babylon's fall to describe the end of Rome. But unknown to him, God had other plans. Just over two centuries later, God baptized the empire instead of destroying it, and Christianity became its official religion. The author wasn't wrong. He was just trying to give hope to the oppressed in the only way he knew how, by searching the Scriptures.

Chapter 20 concerning the thousand year reign, during which Satan is chained and then released, is one of the strangest passages of the entire Bible. If we have been able to get to the truth behind most of the author's symbols, this one is still a puzzle. Even the fundamentalists get into violent disagreements about it. The author goes on to talk about heaven. Maybe we can ask the meaning of the 1000 year reign when we meet God there!

The Bible ends as it should with the triumph of God. On its first page God brought light out of darkness. Yet how often have people preferred to revert to darkness? But one of the last lines of

Revelation echoes that beginning in Genesis.

It is I, Jesus, who have sent my angel to give you this testimony.... I am the morning star, shining bright.... Let the one who hears say: 'Come.' Let the one who thirsts come forward, and let all who desire it accept the gift of life-giving water (Revelation 22:16-17).

(photo: facing page) "Night will be no more, nor will they need light from lamp or sun, for the Lord God shall give them light, and they shall reign forever and ever" (Revelation 22:5).

Glossary/Index

ADOPTIONISM: Some Christians denied the divinity of Jesus Christ, saying that he was merely human and as such was "adopted" by God as "Son of God" (cf. pp. 88-89).

APOCALYPSE: The Book of Revelation was written in a symbolic language to console and strengthen Christians persecuted by the Romans. The coded style allowed the author to write critically about the Romans without the authorities becoming aware of the criticism (cf. Chapter Thirteen).

BEATITUDES ("Blessed"): The pronouncements of Jesus in Matthew 5:3-12 (Sermon on the Mount) and Luke 6:20-22 (Sermon on the Plain) promised true happiness (blessedness), especially to the poor and exploited. The beatitudes describe the spirituality of the Reign of God (cf. pp. 28, 36).

BODY OF CHRIST: Paul referred to the Church as the Body of Christ to signify the unity of its members with Christ, the Head, and of the members with one another. As in a physical body, all members are interdependent, each functioning for the good of the whole. The same term, Body of Christ, is used for the Eucharist, the true presence of Jesus Christ under the appearance of bread and wine (cf. pp. 45, 68, 69,76, 80).

CHURCH: In the New Testament, "Church" usually refers to the local assembly of those who believe in Jesus Christ and are united in his name. This organized fellowship is called by various names such as the "Way" and the "Body of Christ" (cf. pp. 16, 68-69; and the Featurette, "Letter to the Churches," on Page 110).

CIRCUMCISION: The ceremonial practice of cutting off the foreskin of the male organ was common among ancient peoples. Israel adopted the rite as a token of its covenant with God as well as a sign of membership within the chosen people (cf. pp. 24, 45, 60, 71-72).

COVENANT: The Hebrew Scriptures describe a number of agreements, contracts, testaments or promises of loving partnership on the part of God with Israel, making them God's priestly people, a holy nation (Exodus 19:6). The people were obliged to observe the Law, and God promised to reward their fidelity. This Old Testament relationship was perfected and extended to all peoples by Jesus Christ in the New Testament (cf. page 8).

DOCETISM: Some Christians denied that Jesus was truly human, claiming that Jesus only "appeared" to have a human body. (cf. page 113).

ECUMENISM: The word means "the whole wide world" and refers to a movement to reunite all Christian Churches (cf. pp. 103-7).

ESCHATOLOGY ("The study of the last things"): This part of theology traditionally studied Christian belief regarding death, heaven, hell, purgatory, the resurrection of the body, and the second coming of Christ.

ESSENES: This Jewish sect lived a monastic-like life in strict observance of the Law. Their center near the Dead Sea was occupied by Roman soldiers in the second part of the first century A.D. Prior to that occupation, the Essenes hid their vast library which was rediscovered in 1948 and named, "The Dead Sea Scrolls." Their prominent leader was called, "The Teacher of Righteousness." They awaited two Messiahs: one spiritual and one political (cf. page 85, and the Featurette, "Qumran" on Page 104).

FUNDAMENTALISM: This term refers to those Christians who interpret the Bible literally, as if Scripture had been dictated word for word by God to human secretaries (in English!) (cf. pp. 62, 112, and Chapter Thirteen).

GOSPEL ("Good News"): A term applied to the accounts of Jesus' ministry attributed to Matthew, Mark, Luke and John. But in its fullest sense Gospel is the proclamation of God's active concern in human history to reconcile and transform all peoples through Jesus Christ into a single family of brothers and sisters: the Reign of God. The Gospel is a message always demanding a human response (cf. pp. 9-10, 13, 16, 25, 76-7, 103).

KINGDOM: cf. REIGN OF GOD.

LAW: The Law of Moses refers to several things. In general, it means the first five books of the Bible, which are attributed to Moses and which summarize Israel's obligations in fulfilment of the Covenant, especially regarding worship and morality. Synagogue services included a continual reading of these books. The Ten Commandments are part of the Law. As time went on, the Law became increasingly associated with the commentaries of rabbis on the Law. These dealt with minute aspects of daily life. Jesus observed the Law but condemned its being reduced to the kind of minute regulations found in these commentaries. In the writings of Paul, the Law represents a type of spiritual slavery to external observances from which Jesus liberates by his summons to faith and the love of God and neighbor (cf. Torah.) (cf. pp. 24-29, 42-45, 60, 69-73, 77, 88-90, 96, 102).

MESSIAH ("One who has been anointed"): This term refers to Israel's kings, for example, David, who were anointed in the name of God. Gradually, prophets began to speak of a "future" son of David who would restore Israel and establish a "new" Covenant. The Greek translation for messiah is "Christos," which became a title for Jesus - "Jesus (the) Christ (anointed one)" (cf. pp. 19, 25, 35, 60).

PAROUSIA ("Arrival"): This refers to the second coming of Jesus Christ in glory at the end of the world when all Christian hopes will be fulfilled. The early Christians expected Jesus' coming to take place within their own lifetime (cf. pp. 61, 63-64).

PHARISEES: The name probably means the "separated (perfect) ones." This sect within Judaism was known for its zeal for the strict observance of the Law and of the rabbinical traditions. This lay group was opposed to the priests' party as well as to the common people, who were generally ignorant of the Law. Jesus condemned the insincerity and hypocrisy of the Pharisees (cf. pp. 18, 29, 36, 45).

PROPHET ("One who speaks on behalf of God"): Usually this term is understood as referring to one who foretells the future, but that is too narrow a definition. Old Testament prophets are often called "seers," that is, one who guides or teaches Israel according to the will of God. They do this as much by their actions as by their words. Their followers are sometimes referred to as "sons of prophets." Prophecy in the New Testament is considered to be a charism to be honored within the community (cf. pp. 18, 29, 35, 44, 61, 116).

REIGN OF GOD: Jesus' central teaching about the "Kingdom" (wherever God rules) dealt with the presence and rule of God within individuals, within groups, and within society as a whole, including the relationship of human beings toward all of creation. Characteristics of the Reign include: fraternity, justice, mercy and peace. The Holy Spirit brings about this transformation (new creation) within history - as a process moving toward full realization at the end of time (cf. pp. 25, 63).

SABBATH: The "seventh" day of the week in Judaism was dedicated to rest, worship and religious study. One purpose was social - to guarantee a time of rest to laborers. The model proposed was the account of the days of creation in the Book of Genesis in which God "rested on the seventh day." Christians began observing the "first day of the week" (Sunday) in honor of Jesus' resurrection (cf. pp. 18, 24).

SCRIBES ("Writer"): To become a scribe in Israel a man needed formal education in the Law and an official appointment (imposition of hands). The role of scribes was to safeguard doctrinal purity regarding both Scripture and traditional teachings. Jesus condemned many of them for imposing impossible burdens upon the common people, whom the scribes generally considered to be ignorant, inferior and unfaithful (cf. pp. 28-29).

SON OF MAN: (Cf. the Featurette, Page 21).

SYNAGOGUE: Every Jewish community was allowed to have an assembly building which served for worship, study, judgment, and as a library. Separate galleries were provided for men and women. The principal services, which were directed by elders, took place on the Sabbath. Every synagogue contained scrolls of the Scriptures and the eight-branched candle, the Menorah (cf. pp. 35, 49-50, 59-60).

SYNOPTIC GOSPELS: The Gospels according to Matthew, Mark and Luke are called the "Synoptics" (Greek = "side by side"), because of their many similarities. Matthew and Luke borrowed from Mark's Gospel as well as from other sources (cf. Page 13).

TEMPLE: The center of Jewish worship and the only place of sacrifice was the temple in Jerusalem. First built by Solomon (c. 1000 B.C.), it was destroyed about 600 B.C. A second temple was destroyed in 167 B.C., and the third and last temple was built just prior to Jesus' lifetime and was destroyed in 70 A.D. by the Romans. Divisions separated the place of yearly sacrifice (Holy of Holies), the court of the priests, the court of the laity, the court of the women, and finally, the court of the Gentiles (the only place permitted to non-Jews). It was from this last court that Jesus drove out the merchants (cf. Page 107).

TORAH ("Instruction"): This is the general word for law in Judaism, which had both written and oral forms. The written form is the Old Testament which includes a number of "codes" or formalized teachings about faithfulness to God, for example, the Code of the Covenant and the Holiness Code. The oral forms of the Law were rabbinical commentaries on the Old Testament (cf. Law.) (cf. page 28).

Photo Credits

Cover Photo: from **Listen the Clams Are Talking**
        by Emery Tang, OFM
6-7: American Stock Photography
8: Karl Holtsnider
10, 11: United Nations
12: Franciscan Communications (Michael McBlane)
14-15, 16: United Nations
17: Franciscan Communications (Ralph Swanson)
18: Franciscan Communications (Michael McBlane)
19: Anthony Boccaccio
20, 21: Franciscan Communications (Michael McBlane)
22-23: Franciscan Communications
24: Franciscan Communications (Edd Anthony, OFM)
25: Franciscan Communications
27: Eric Wheater (Maryknoll Missioners)
28: Franciscan Communications
29: Eric Wheater (Maryknoll Missioners)
30-31: Catholic Relief Services (Anthony Suau)
32, 33: Franciscan Communications (Michael McBlane)
34-35: Franciscan Communications (Ralph Swanson)
36: Catholic Relief Services (Sewegal)
37, 38: Edd Anthony, OFM
39, 40-41: Catherine Busch
42: Franciscan Communications (Michael McBlane)
43, 44: United Nations
45: Franciscan Communications (Michael McBlane)
46-47: American Stock Photography
48: Catherine Busch
49: Franciscan Communications (Gavin Griffith, OFM)
50: Catherine Busch
51: Franciscan Communications (Catherine Busch)
52: Anthony Boccaccio
53: Maryknoll Missioners (William Scheer, MM)
54: Anthony Boccaccio
55: Franciscan Communications
58-59: Anthony Boccaccio
60: Maryknoll Missioners (S. DeMott)
61: Catherine Busch
62: American Stock Photography
63: NASA
64: Franciscan Communications (Michael McBlane)
65: Anthony Boccaccio
66-67: Catholic Relief Services (Msgr. Coll)
68, 70: Franciscan Communications (Michael McBlane)
71: Catherine Busch
72: Franciscan Communications (Jack Quinn, SJ)
73: American Stock Photography
74-75: Franciscan Communications (Jack Quinn, SJ)
76, 77: United Nations
78: Franciscan Communications (Michael McBlane)
79: Anthony Boccaccio
81: Franciscan Communications
82: United Nations
84: Maryknoll Missioners (A. Scheid, ALM)
86-87: Edd Anthony, OFM
88: Maryknoll Missioners (E. Baskerville, MM)
89: Edd Anthony, OFM
90: Bill Barrett

91: Catherine Busch
92: Franciscan Communications (Jack Quinn, SJ)
93: Bill Barrett
94-95: Mark Chodzko
96: Hale Observatories
97: Anthony Boccaccio
98: Maryknoll Missioners (M. Sandoval)
99: Franciscan Communications (Michael McBlane)
100-101: Catherine Busch
102: Maryknoll Missioners (R. R. Saucci, MM)
103: Maryknoll Missioners
104: Franciscan Communications
105: Maryknoll Missioners (J. Padula)
106: Catherine Busch
108-109: NASA
110: Bill Barrett
111, 112: Franciscan Communications (Michael McBlane)
113: Edd Anthony, OFM
114-115: National Optical Astronomy Observatories
116: United Nations
117, 118, 119: Catherine Busch
120: American Stock Photography
121: Catholic Relief Services (J. Isaac)
122: Edd Anthony, OFM

ILLUSTRATIONS
9: Chart courtesy of St. Mary's Press,
        THE CATHOLIC CHURCH: Our Mission
        in History, 1985, p. 97.
56-57: Map by Linda Rowley

Franciscan Communications, a non-profit organization, seeks to communicate the gospel vision of life in the spirit of St. Francis of Assisi. It has been one of the foremost producers of religious broadcast media in the United States for the past 40 years. Its award-winning TeleKETICS Division continues to serve the audiovisual needs of religious educators, liturgists and pastors, while expanding its ministry into print and publications. Fr. Anthony Scannell, Capuchin, is President of Franciscan Communications. For more information, write to:

Fr. Anthony Scannell, President
Franciscan Communications
1229 S. Santee St.
Los Angeles, CA 90015
(213) 746-2916

AUTHOR: STEPHEN DOYLE, OFM - STL, SSL, was born
in Philadelphia in 1934. After entering the Franciscan Order,
he obtained academic degrees at St. Bonaventure University
(BA), The Catholic University of America (STL and MA), and
the Pontifical Biblical Institute, Rome (SSL). He has taught at
a number of colleges and seminaries in the U.S.A., lectured in
Asia, Europe and Latin America, and written numerous articles
and authored eight books. Stephen Doyle is also well known
through the media, radio and TV, as well as through his
popular biblical lectures on cassettes and video. Hundreds of
seminarians, priests, religious and pilgrims have profited from
his retreats and guided tours to the Holy Land. Presently,
Stephen Doyle is Assistant to the Rector of Tantur, a center for
continuing education and spiritual renewal near Jerusalem.